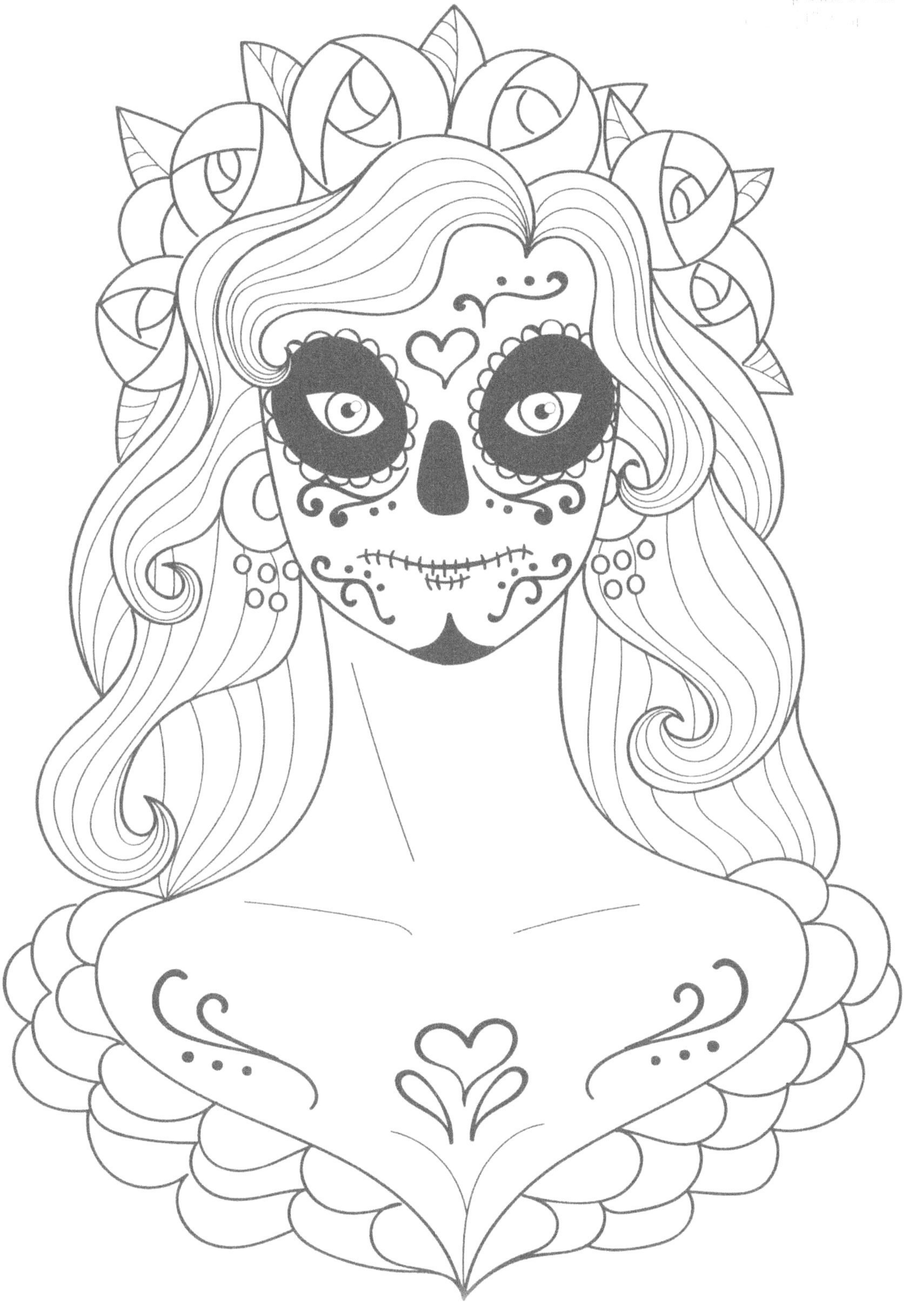

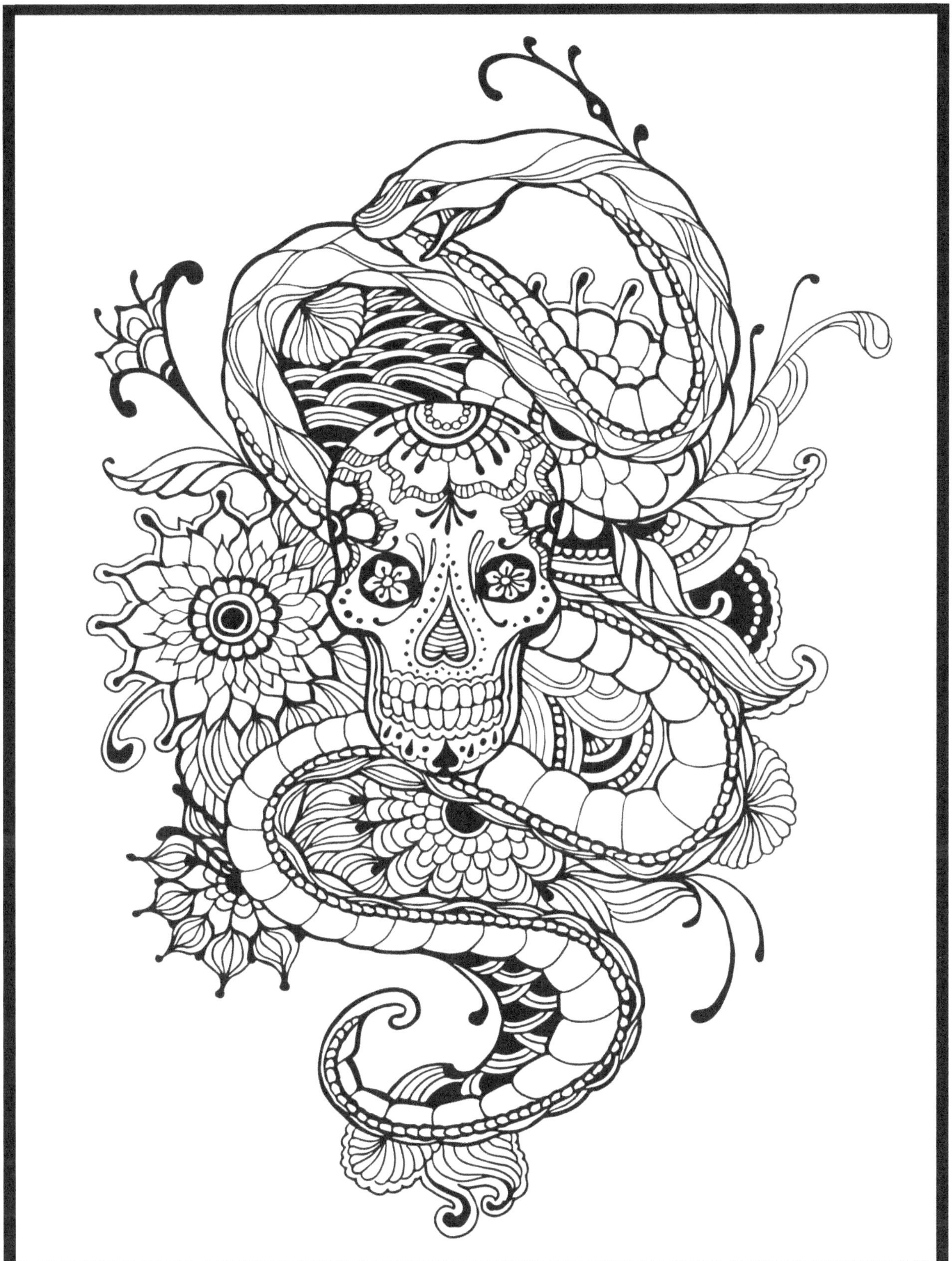

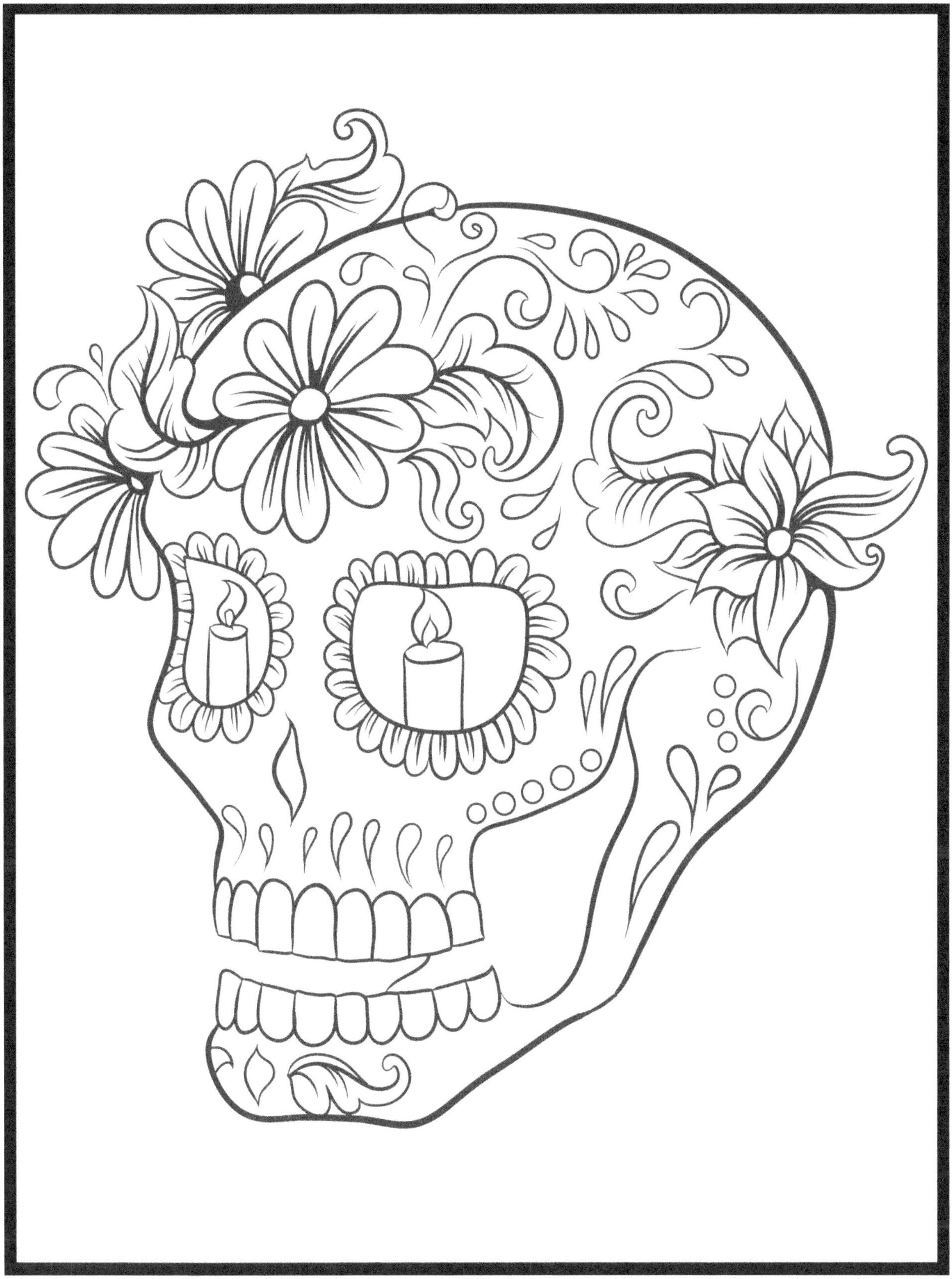

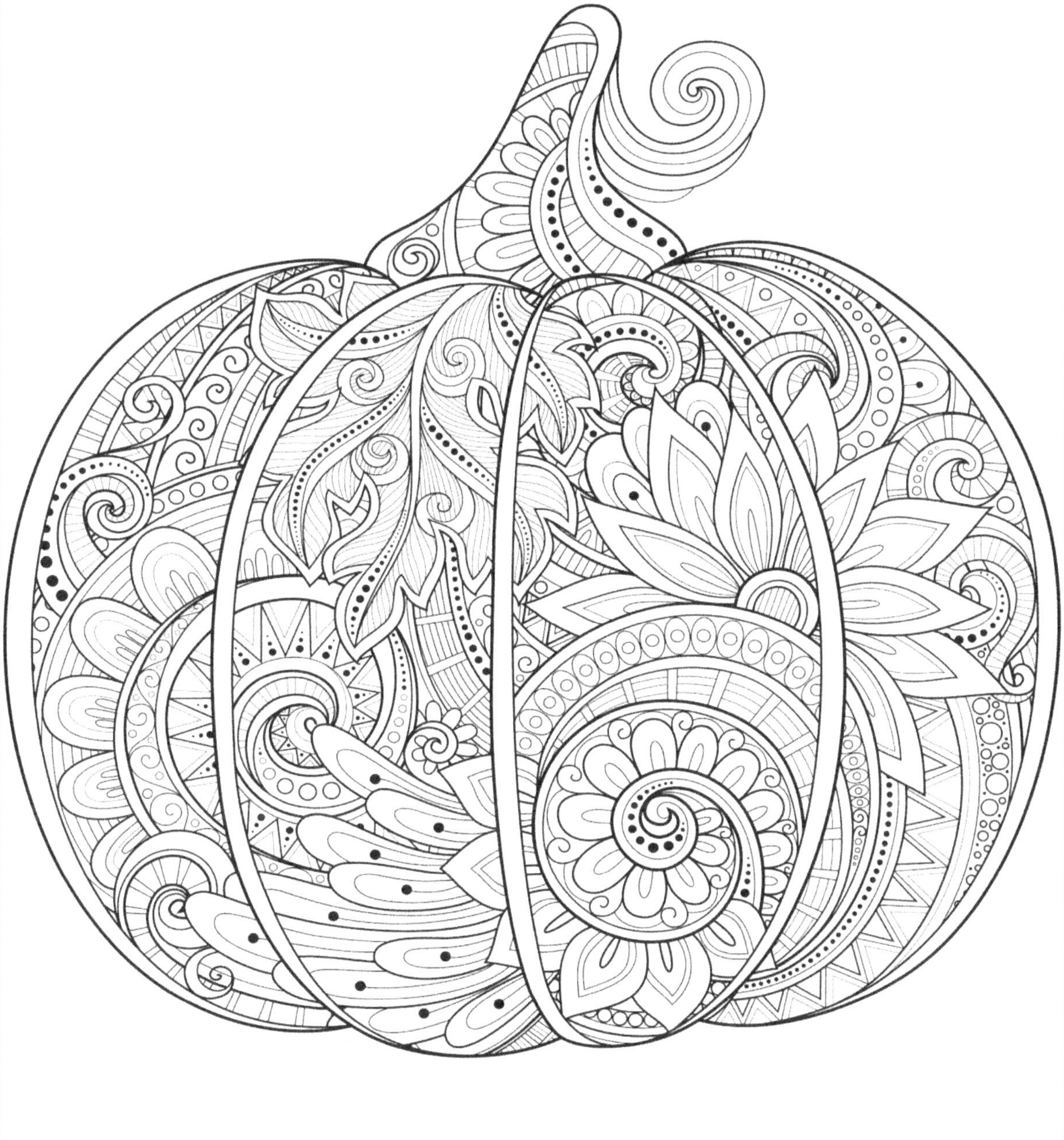

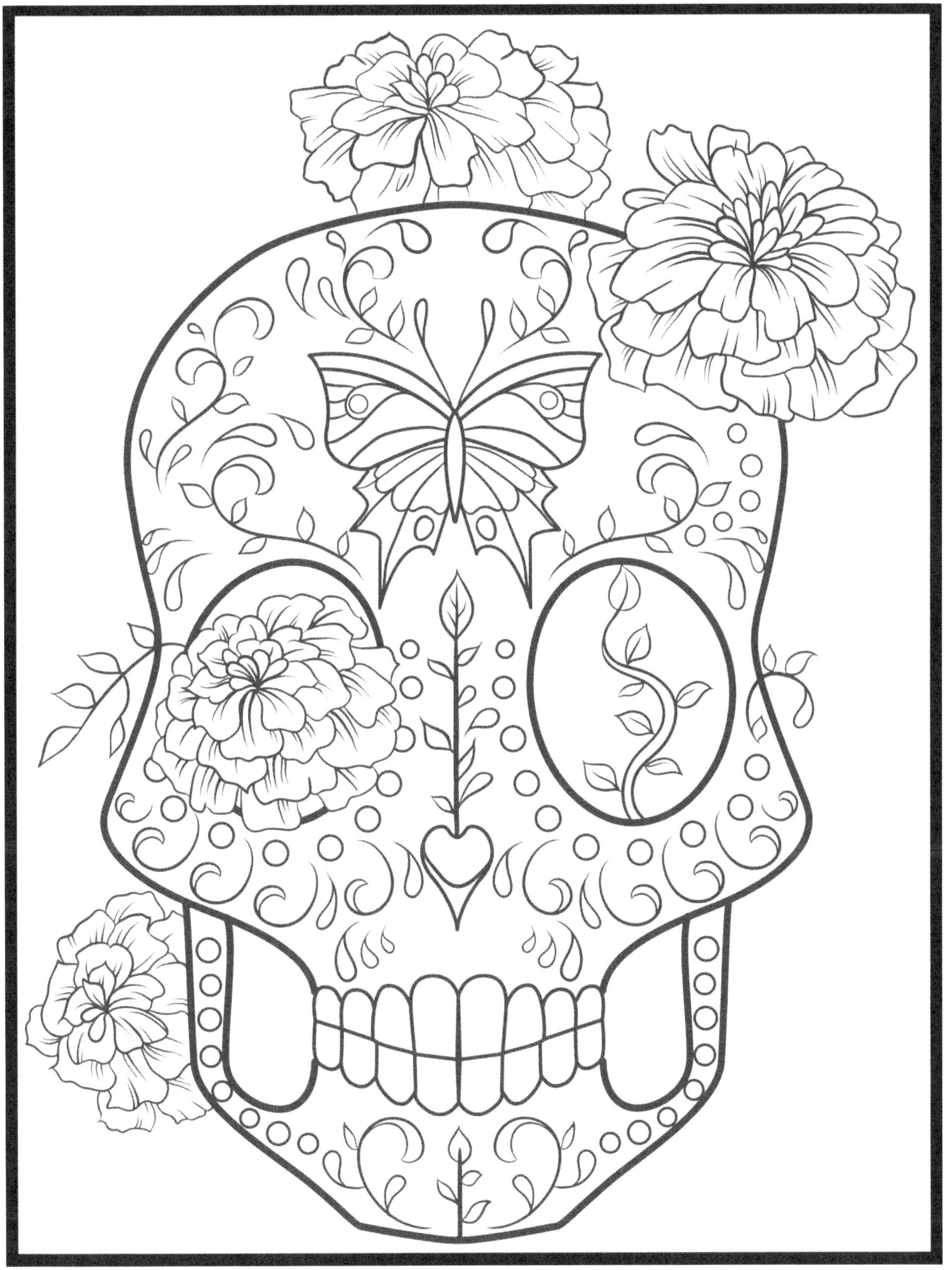

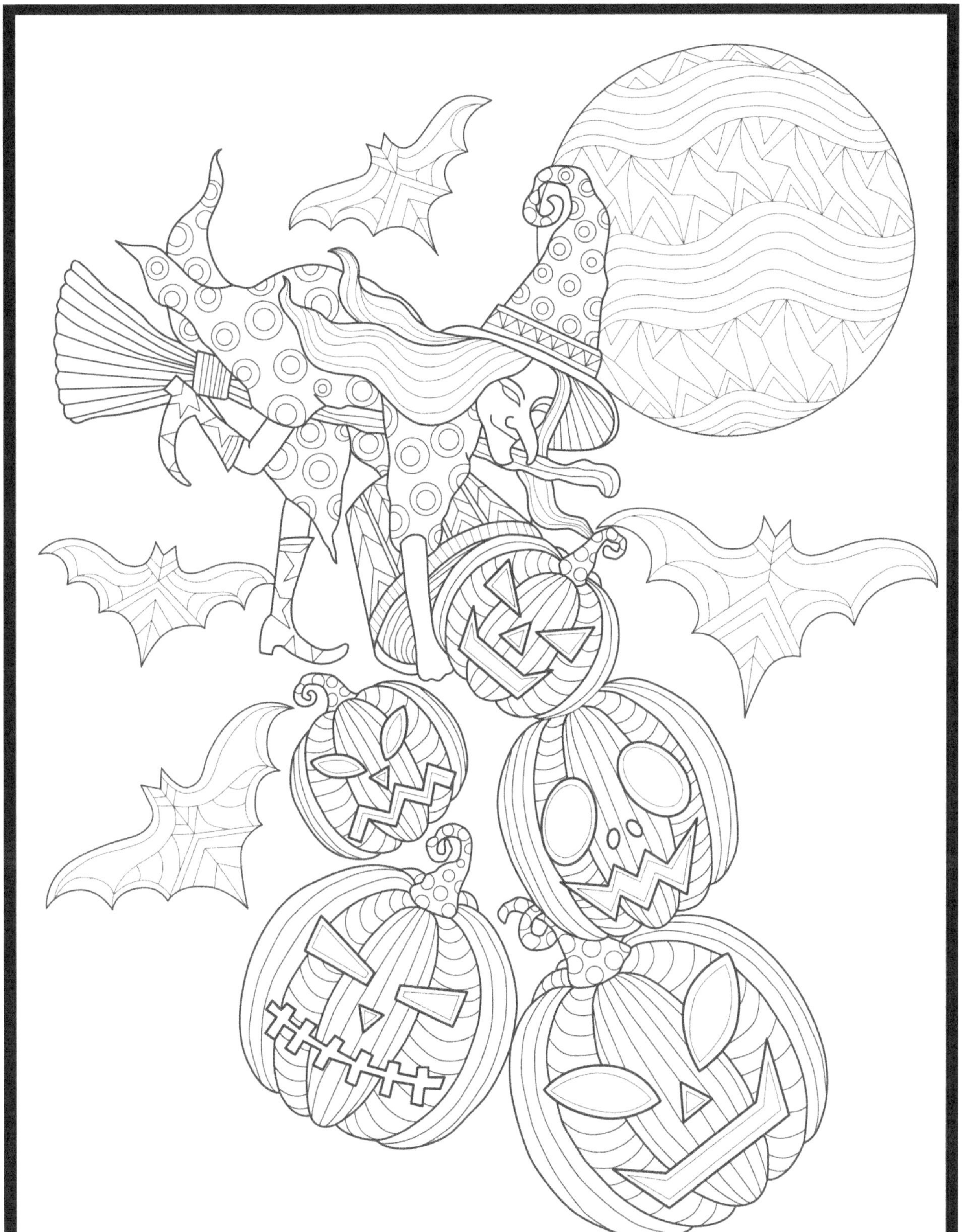

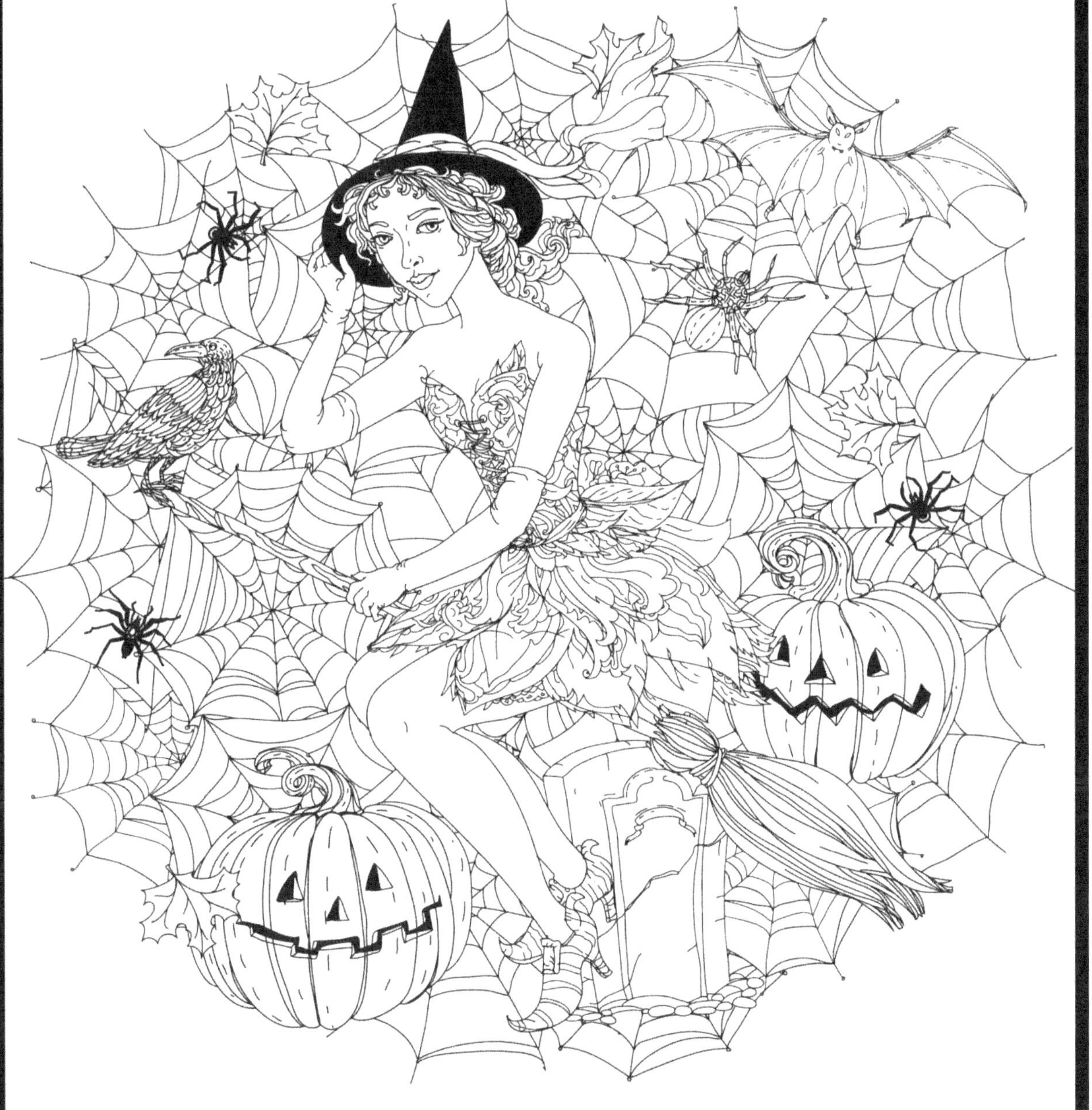

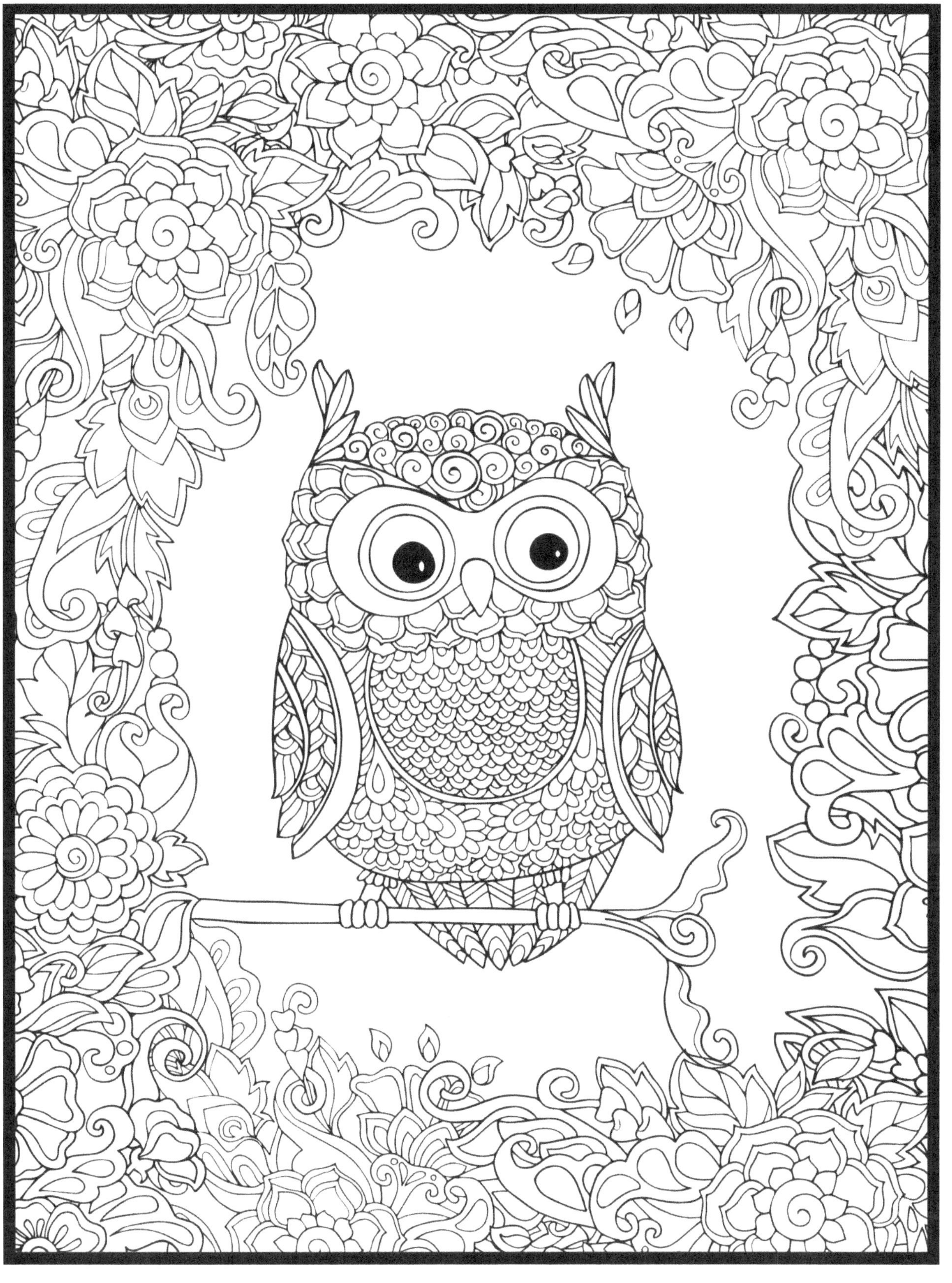

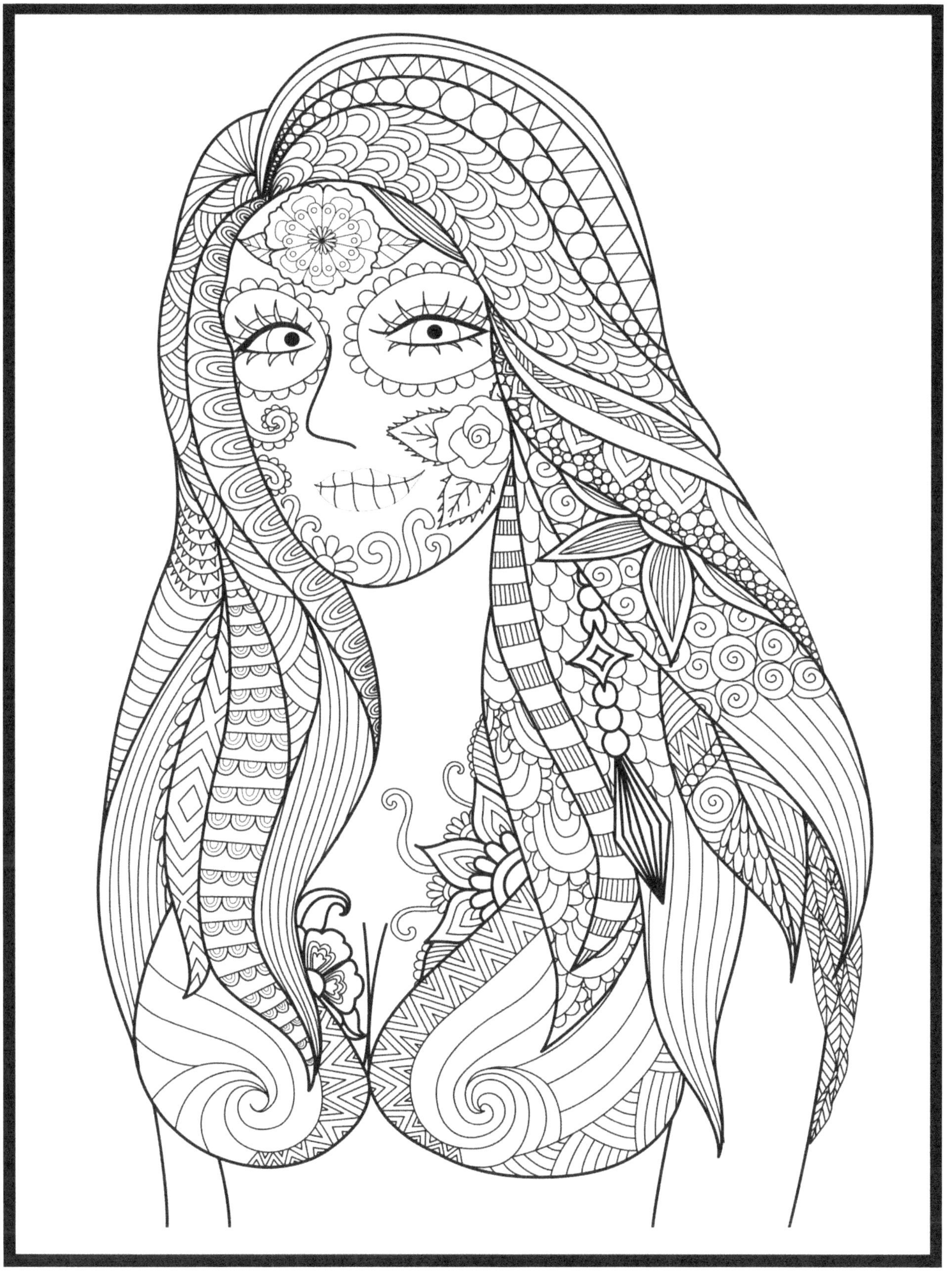

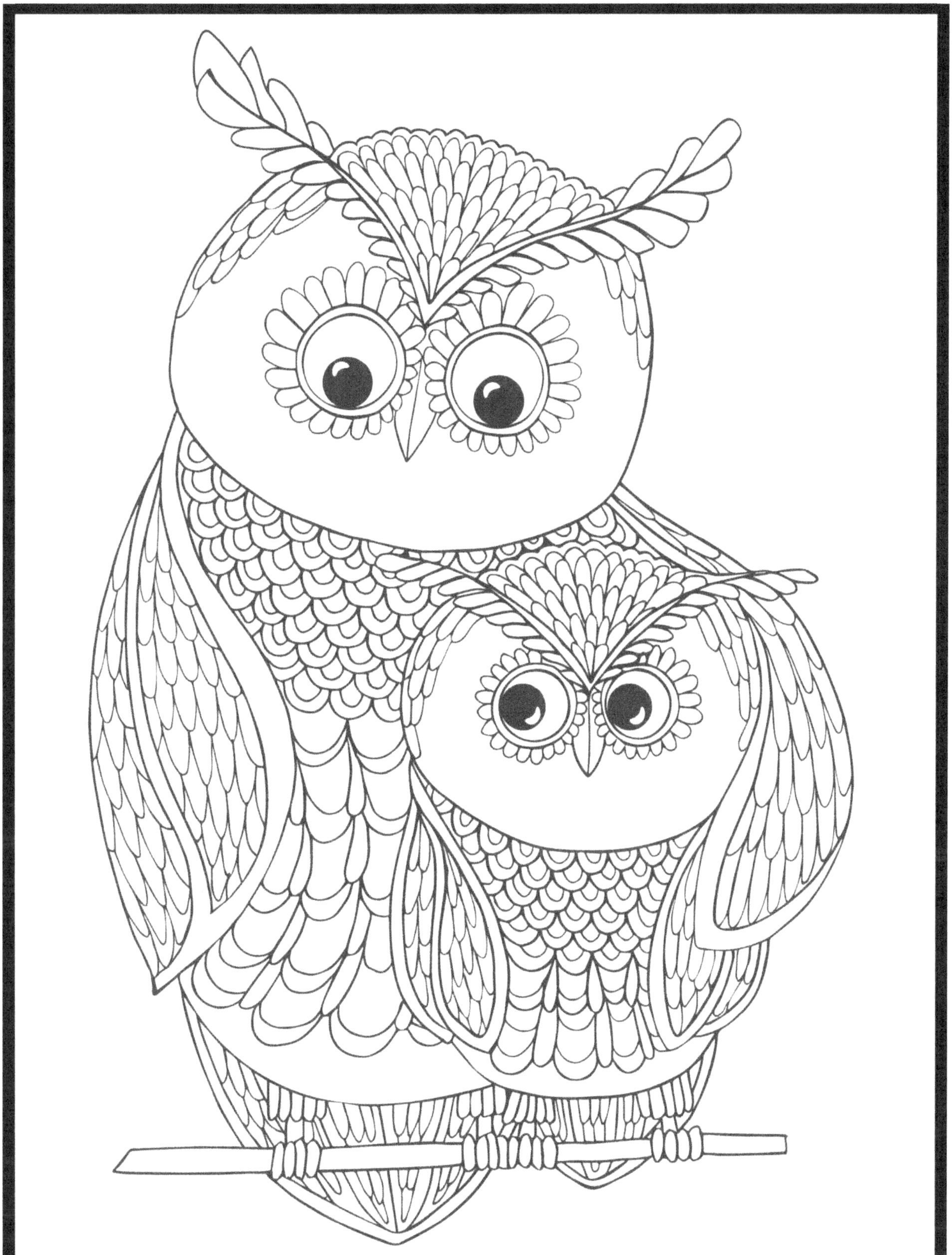

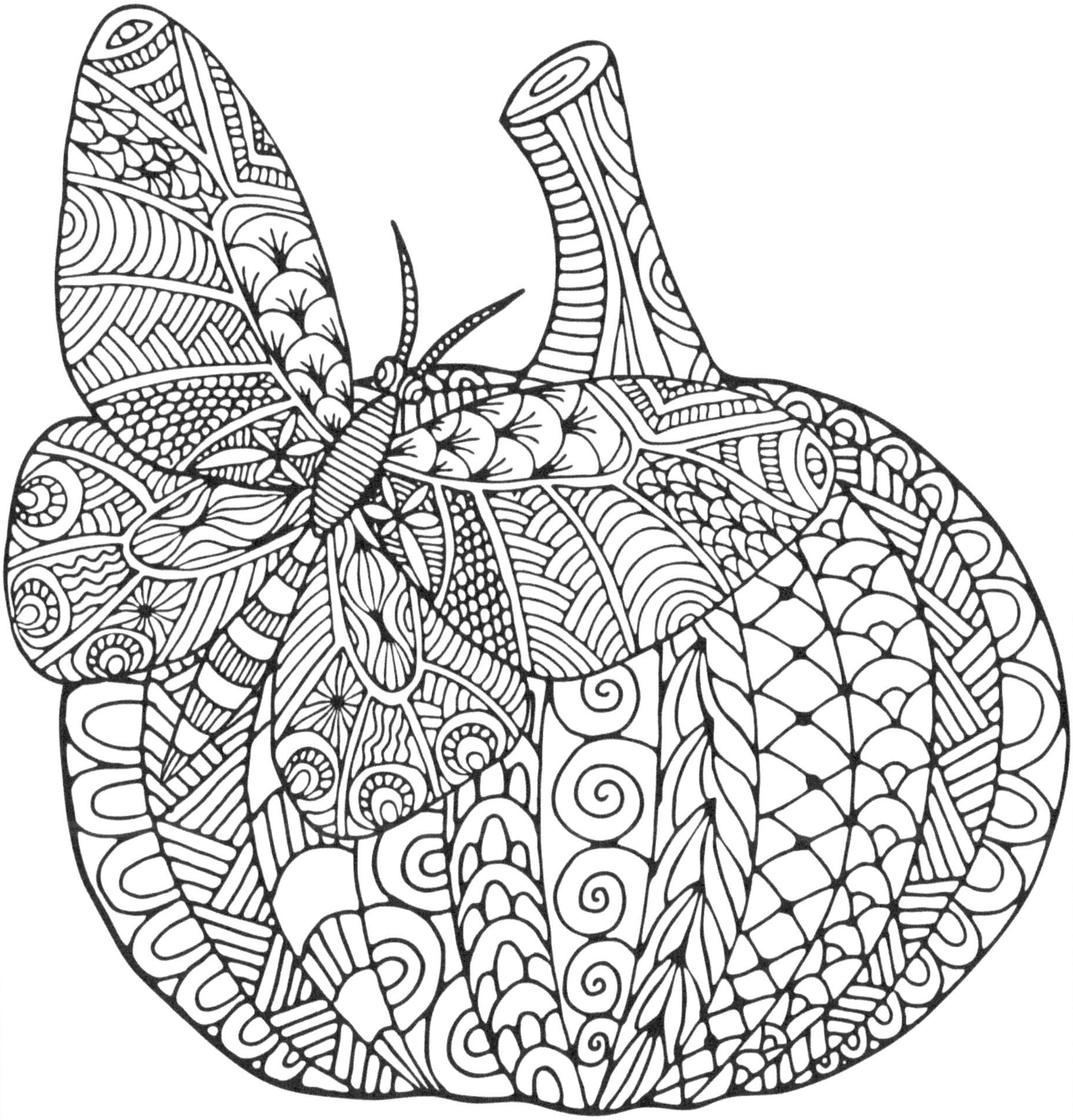

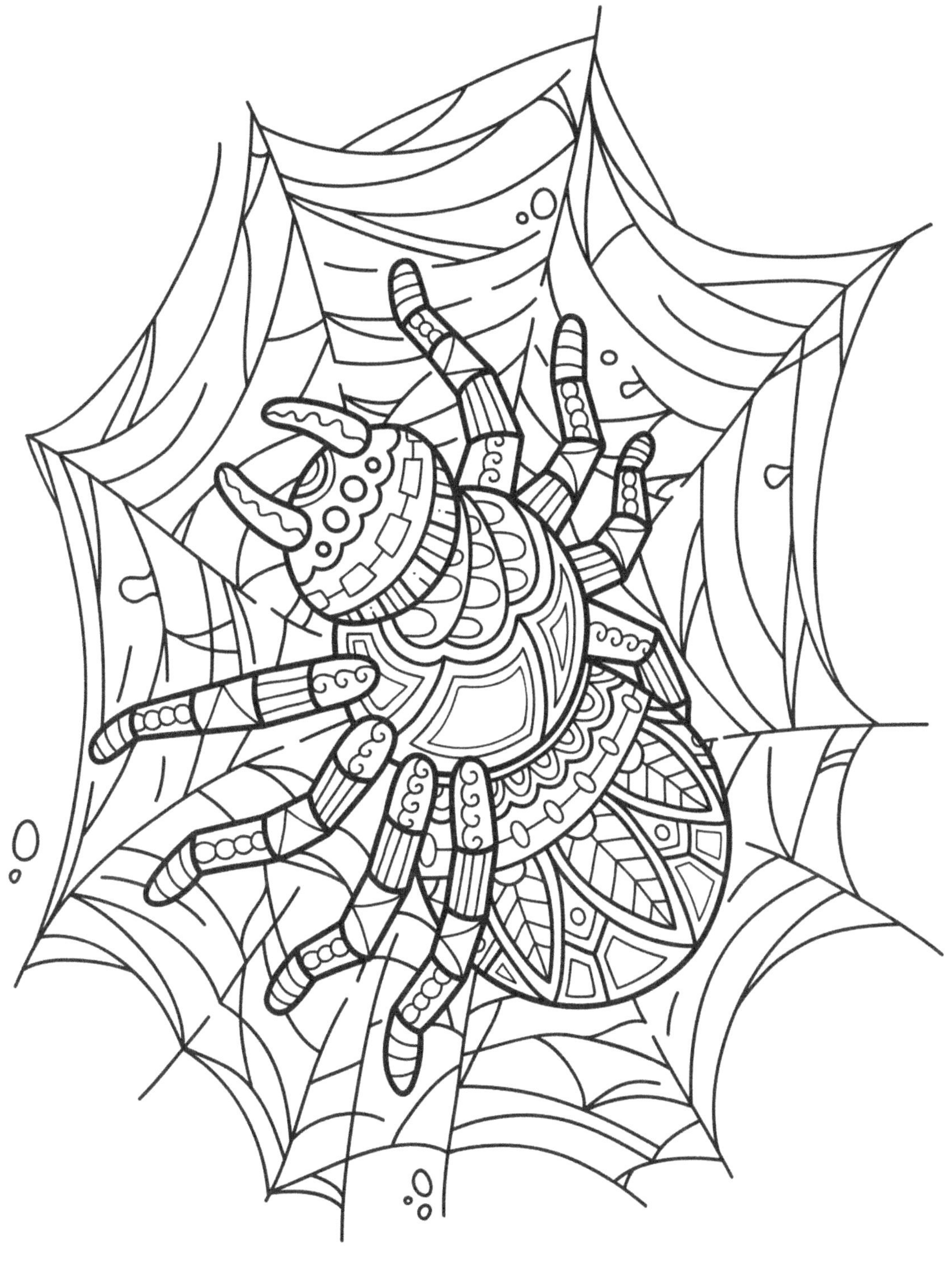

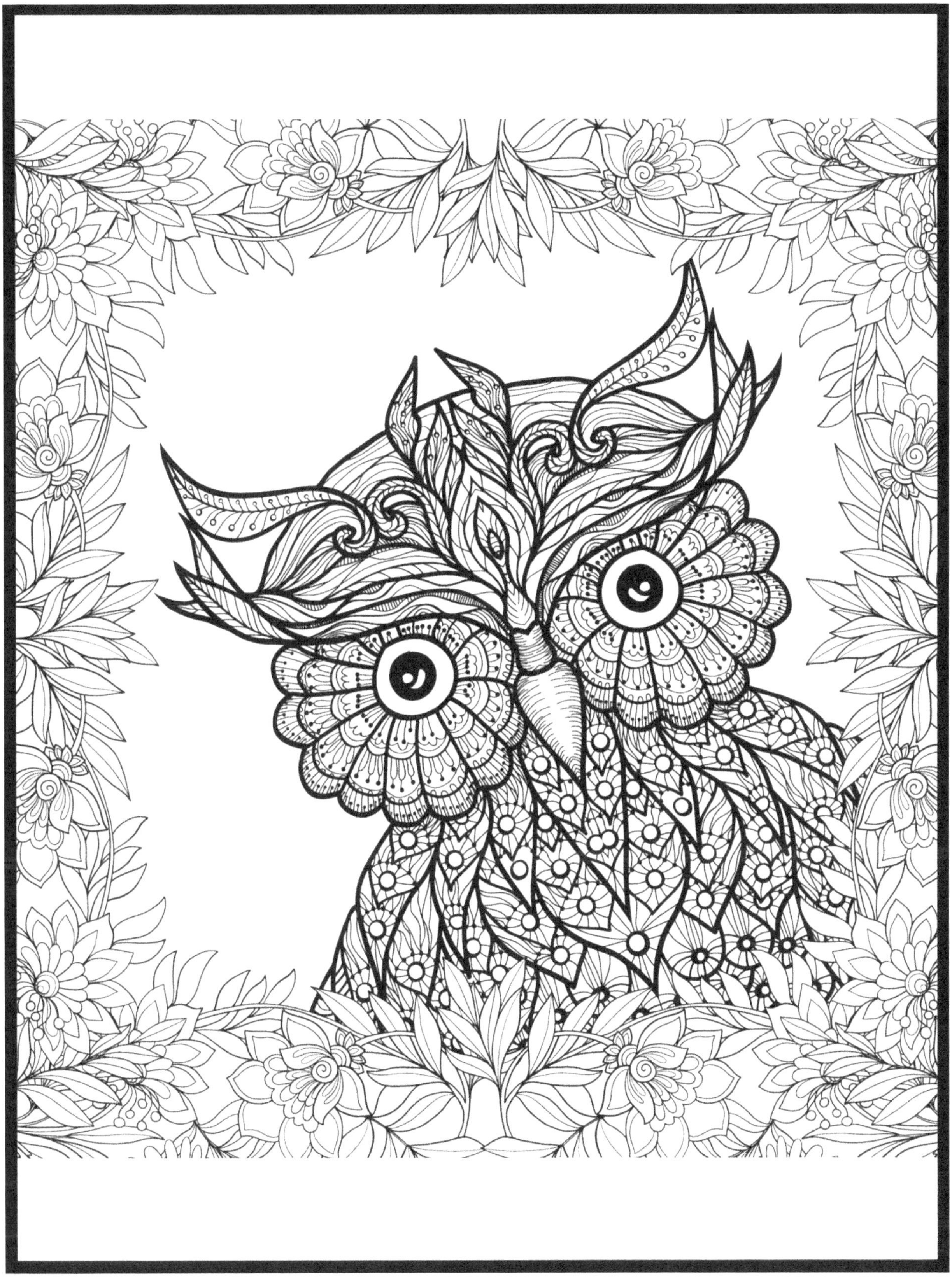

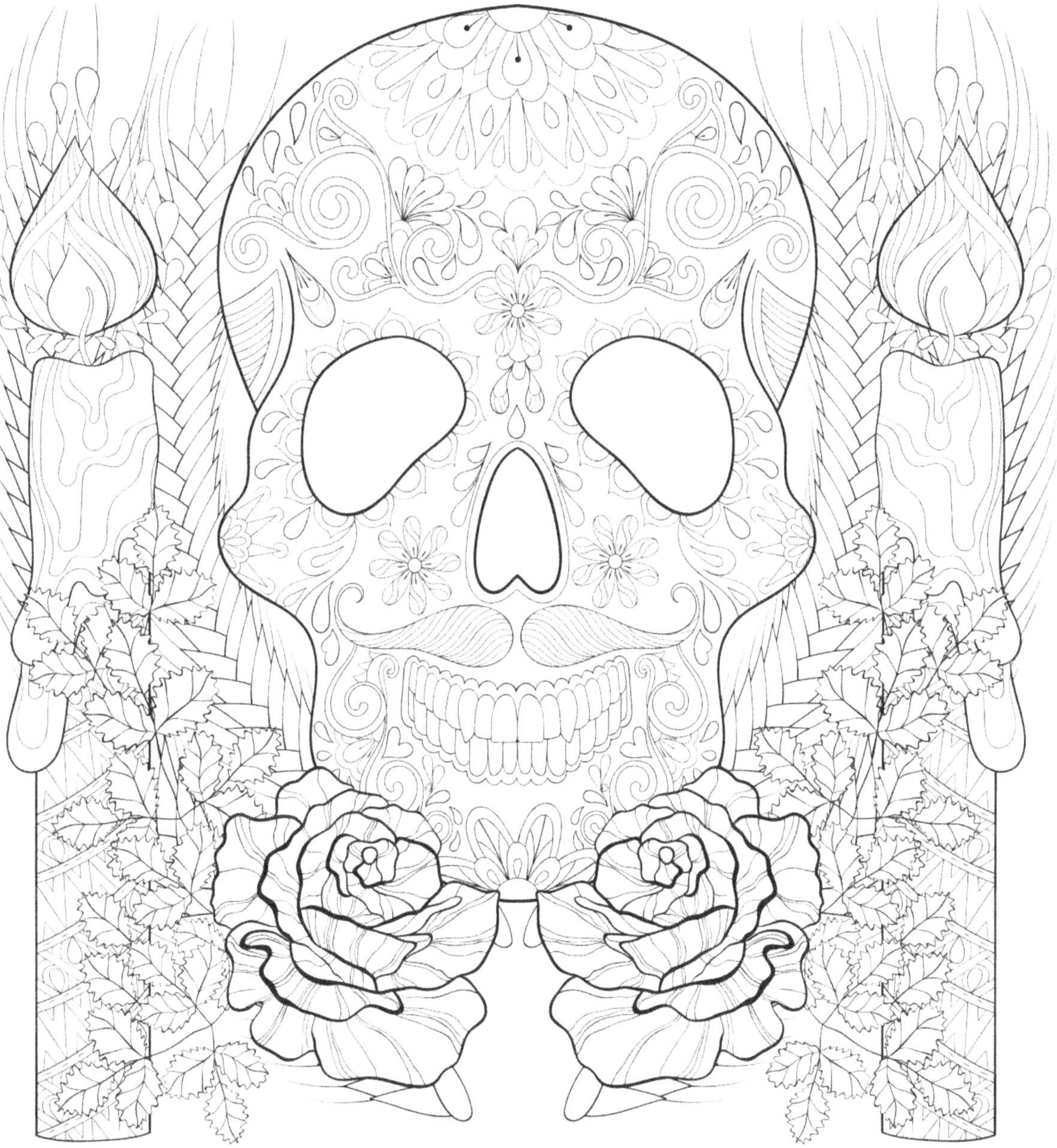

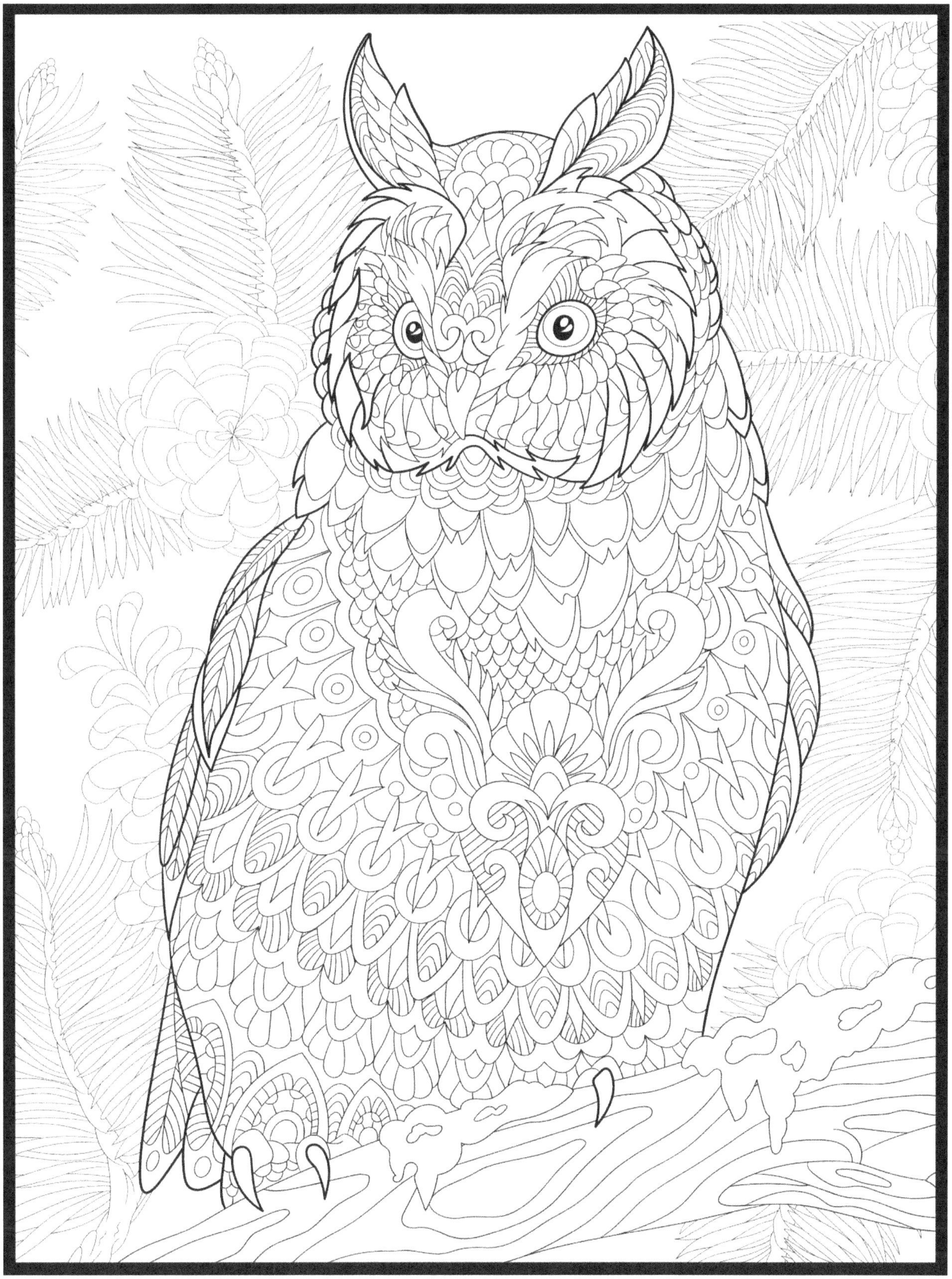

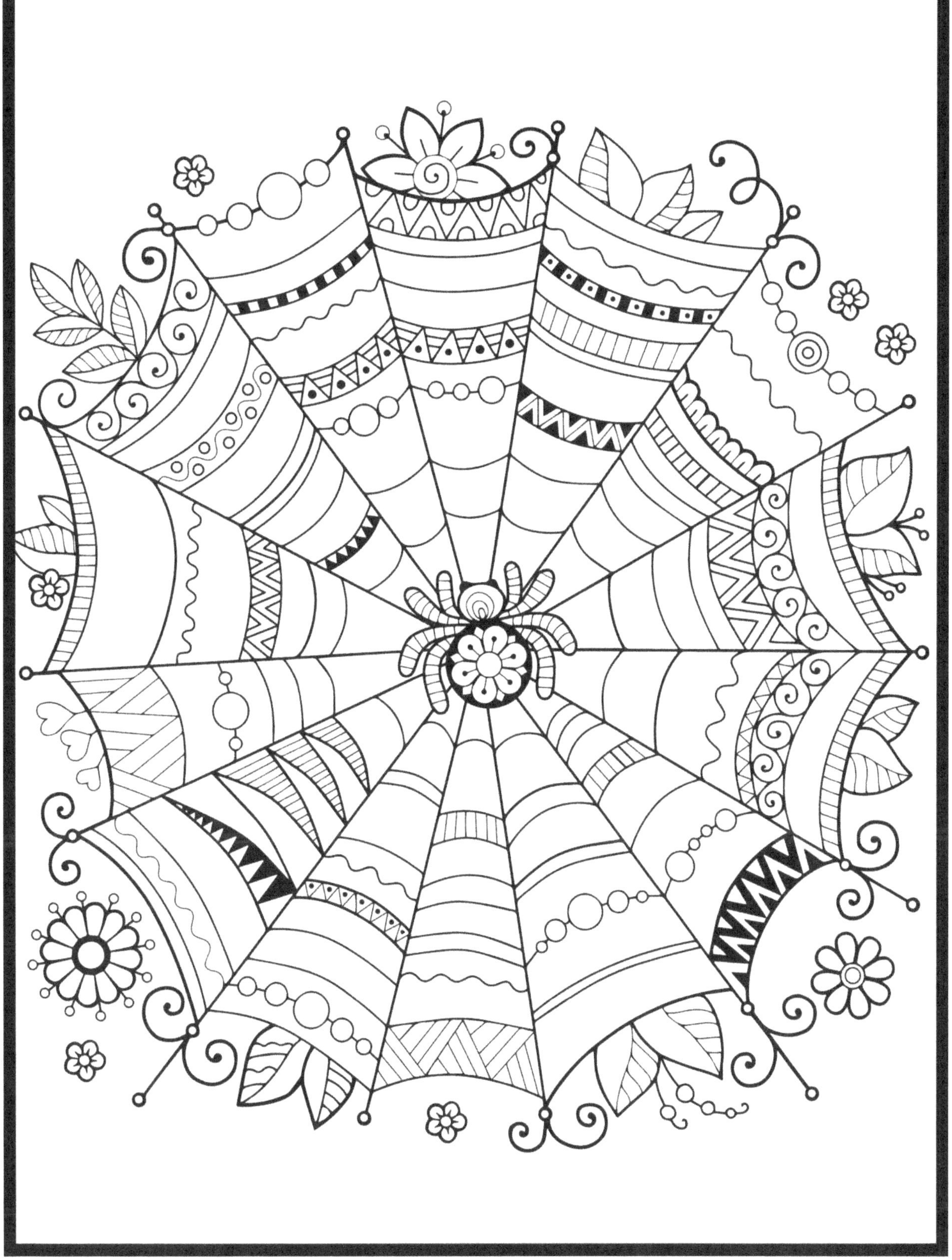

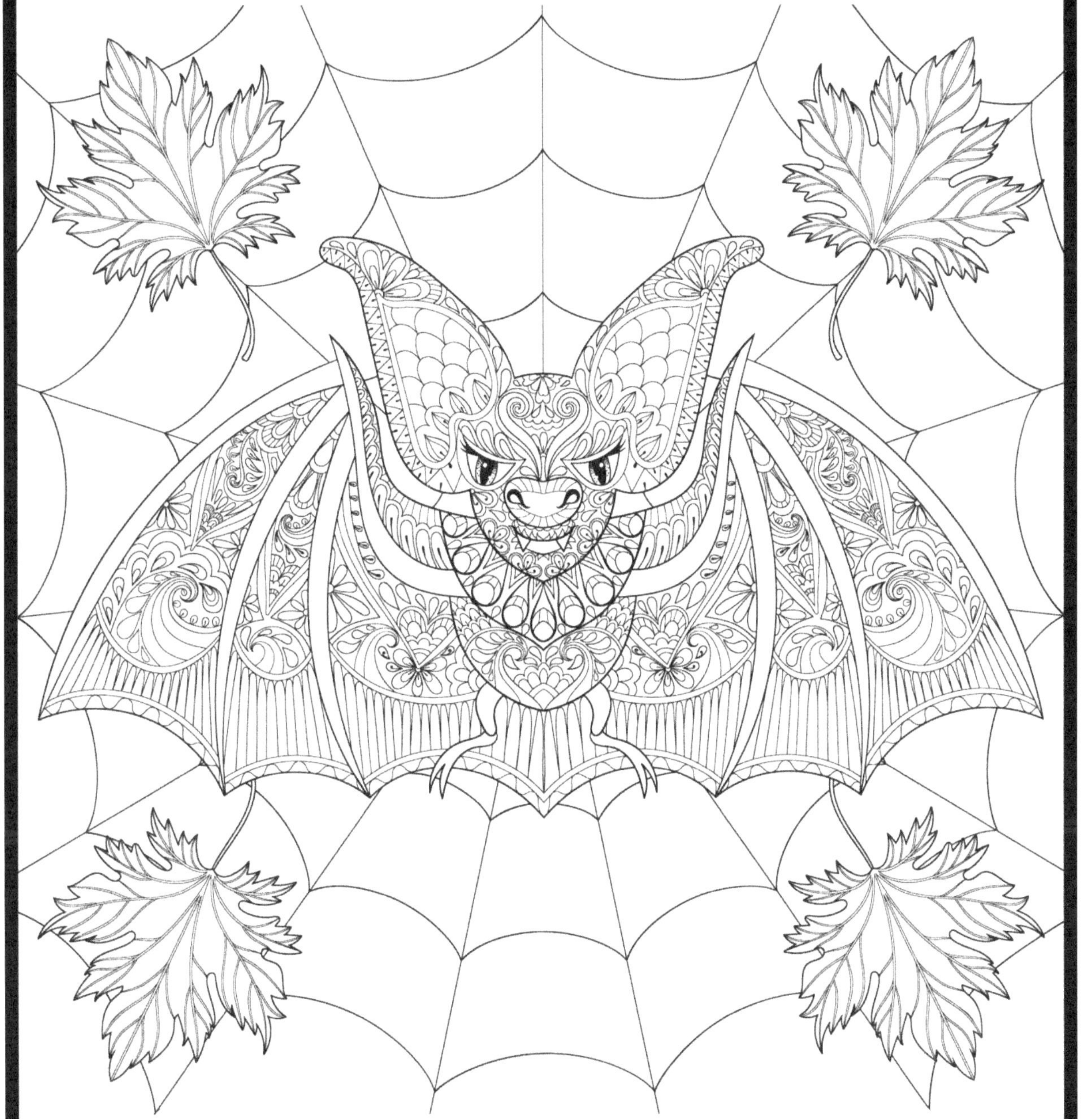

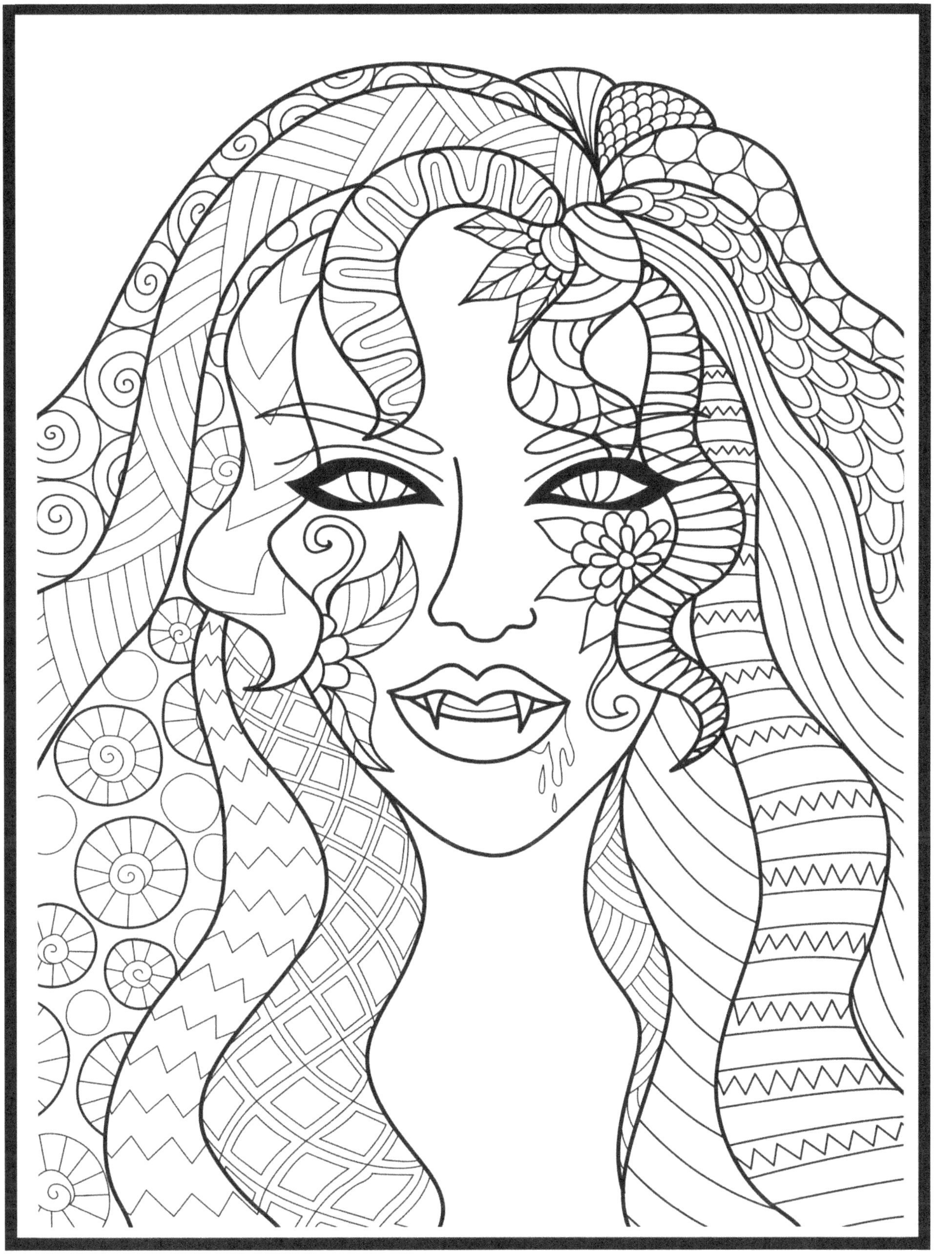

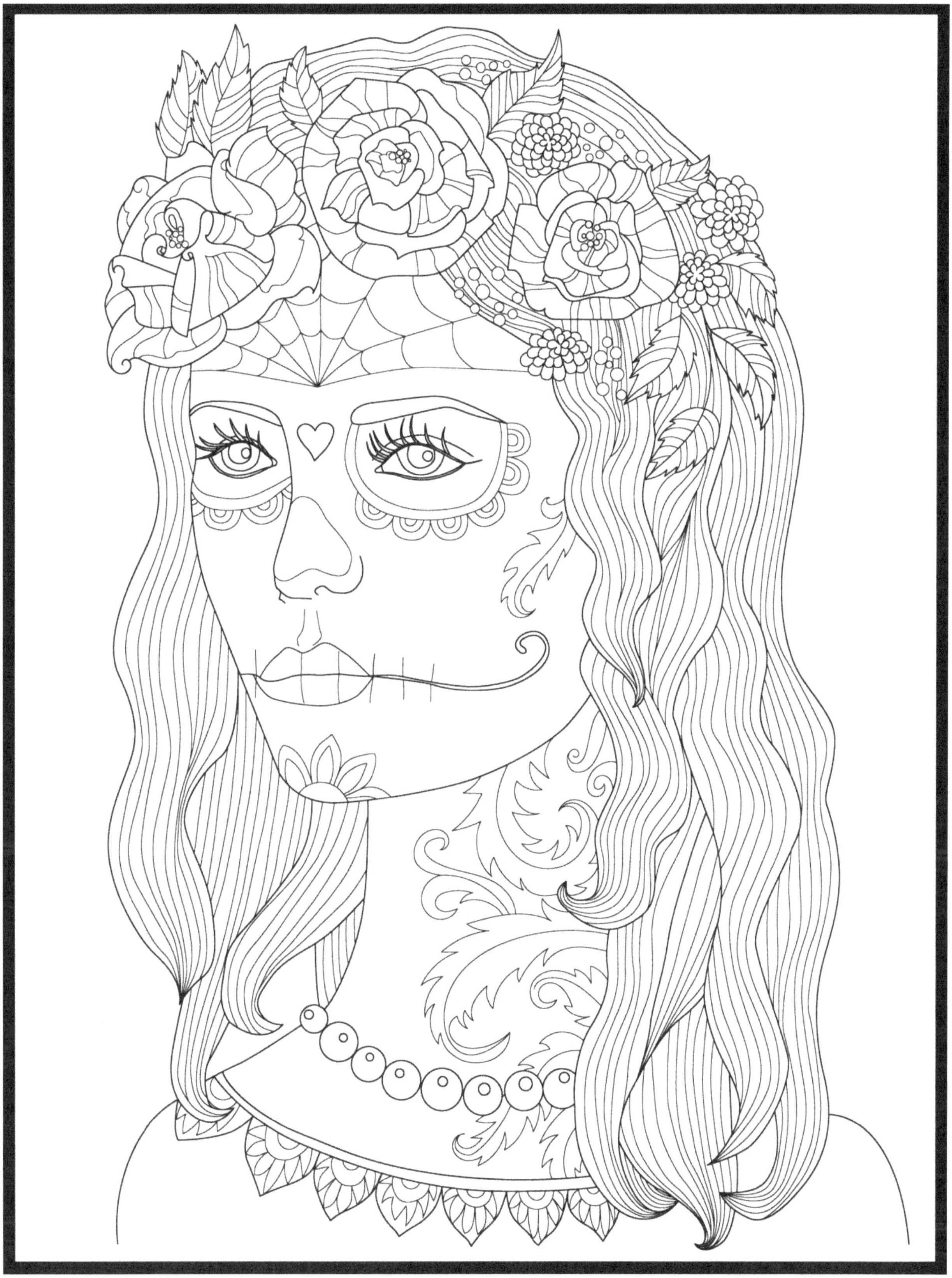

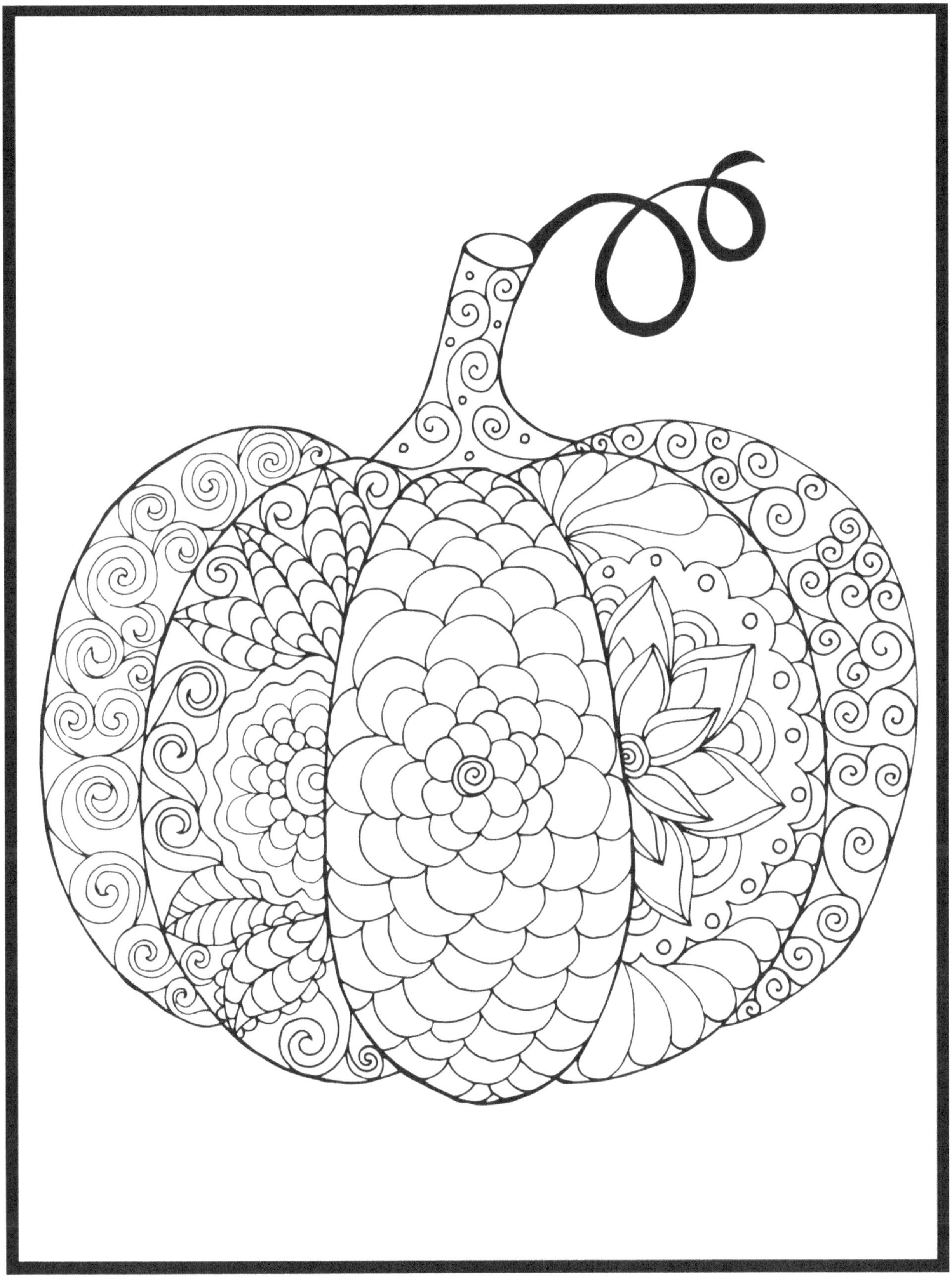

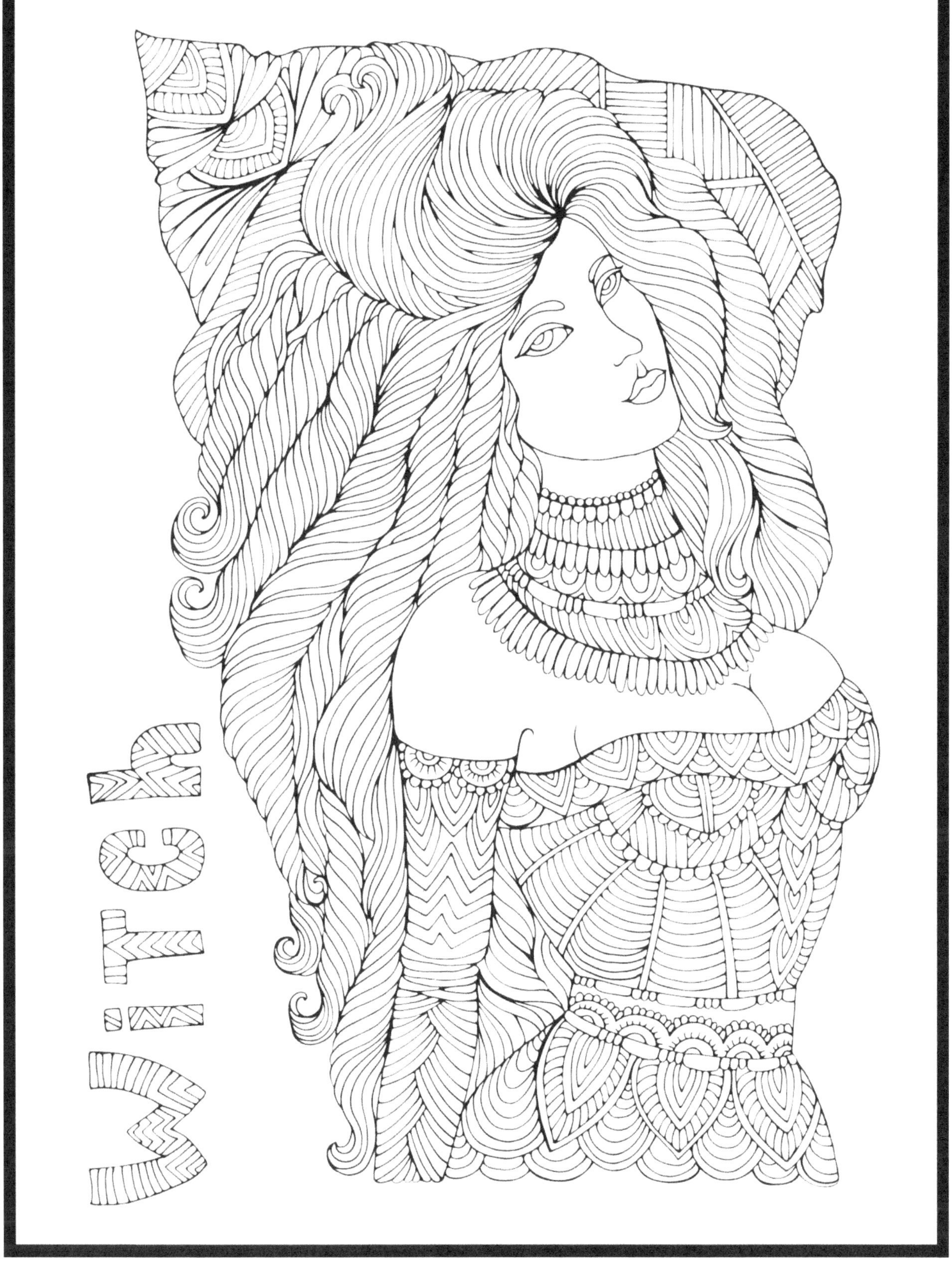
Witch

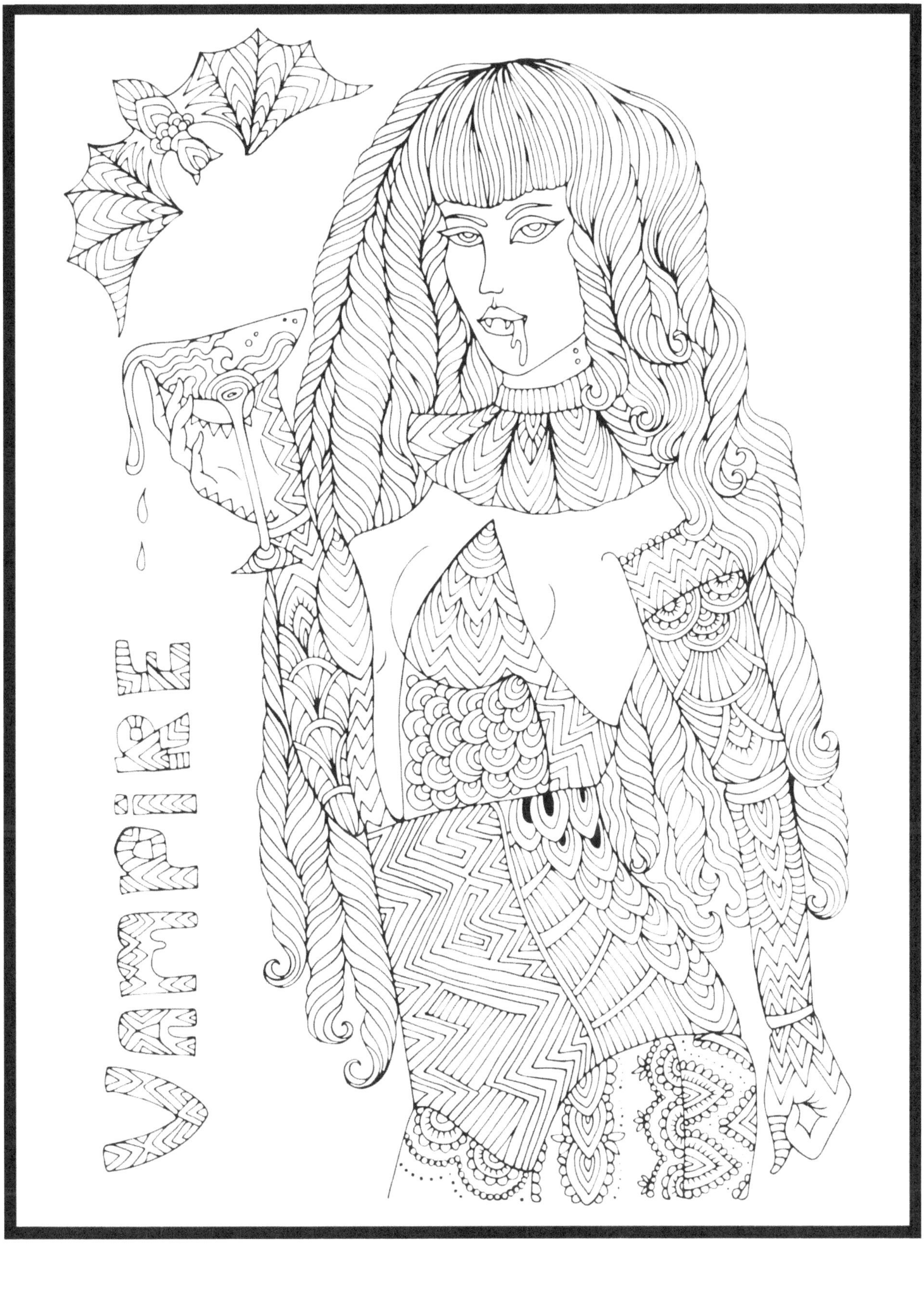
VAMPIRE

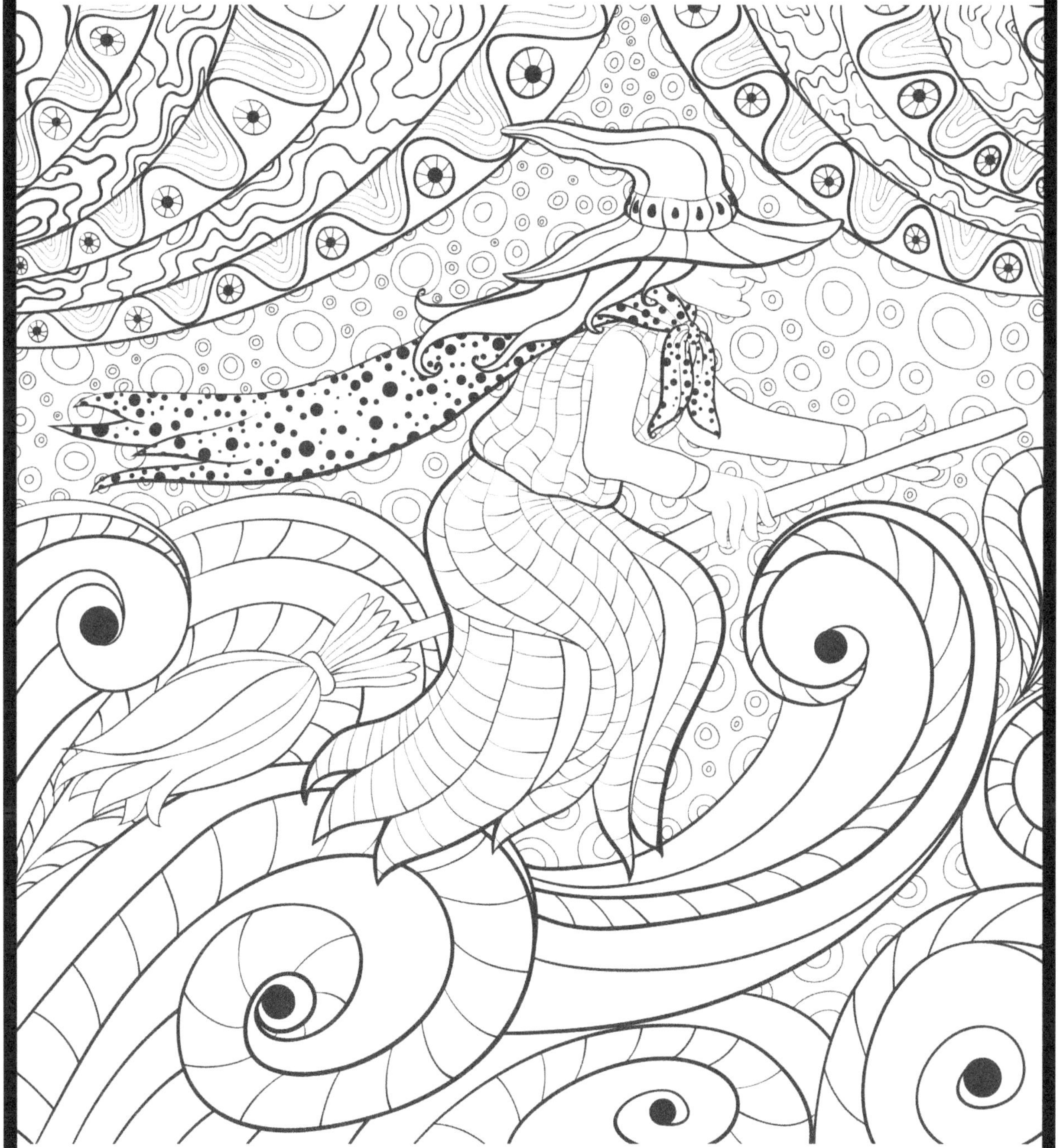

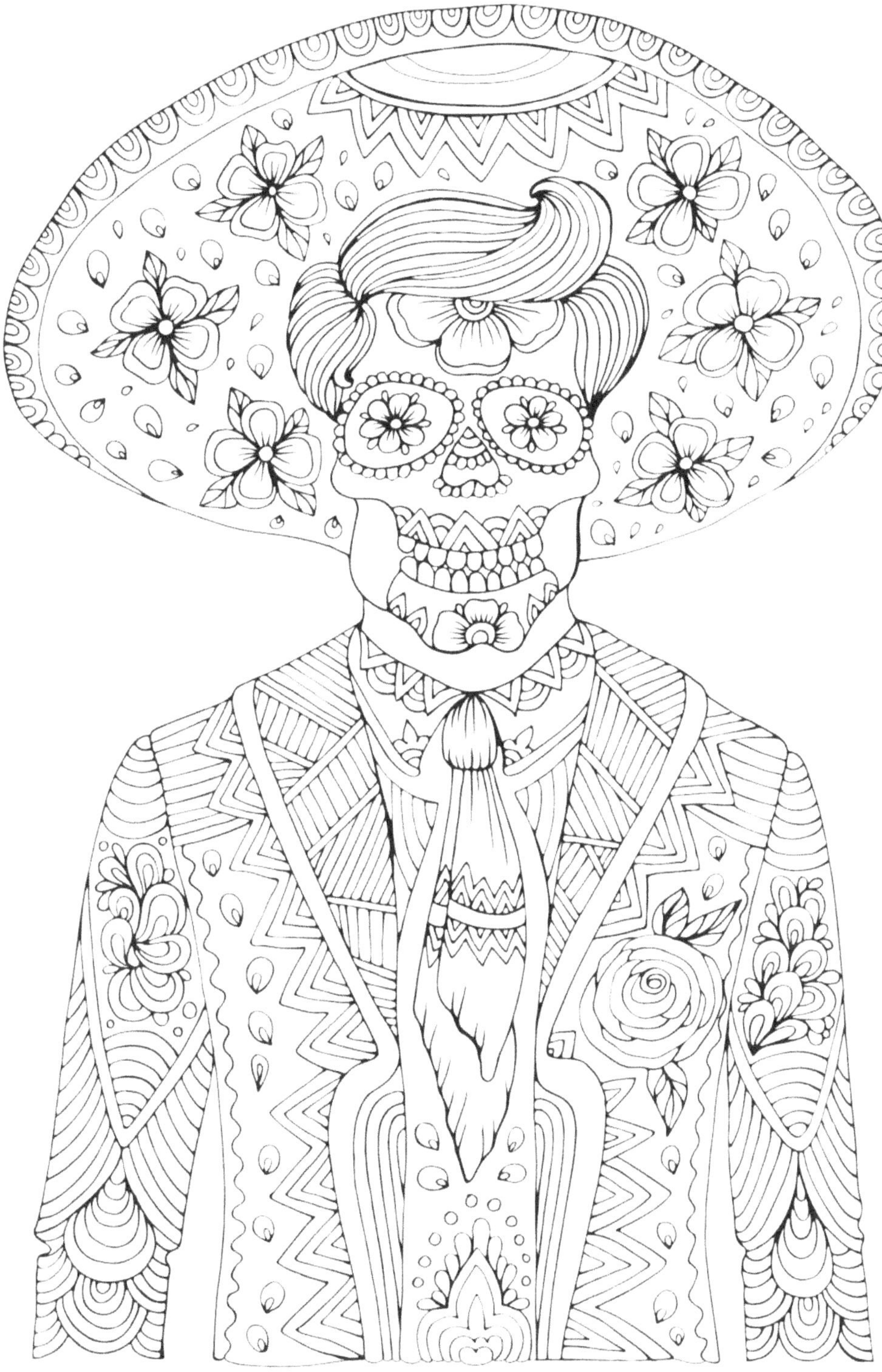

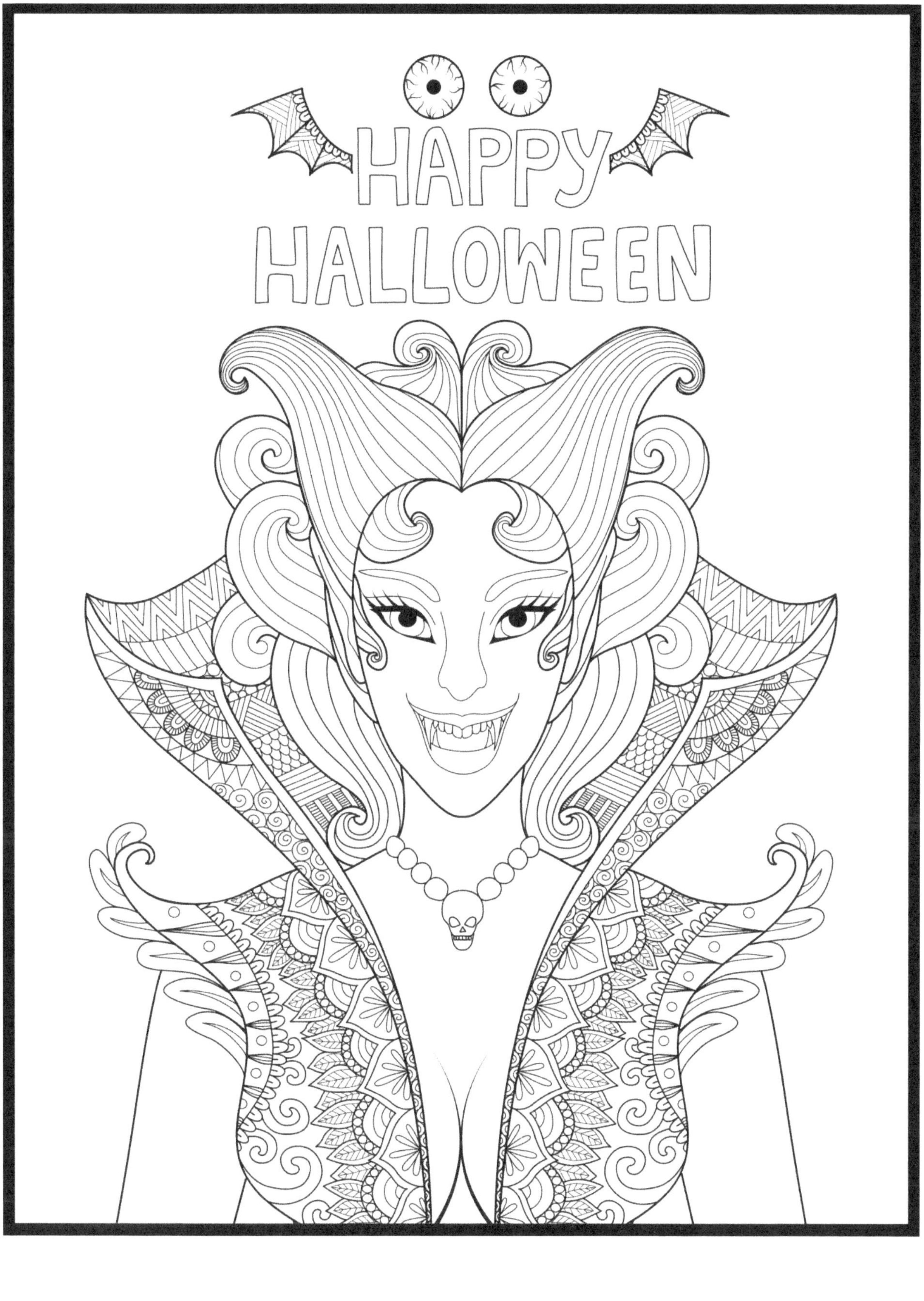
HAPPY
HALLOWEEN

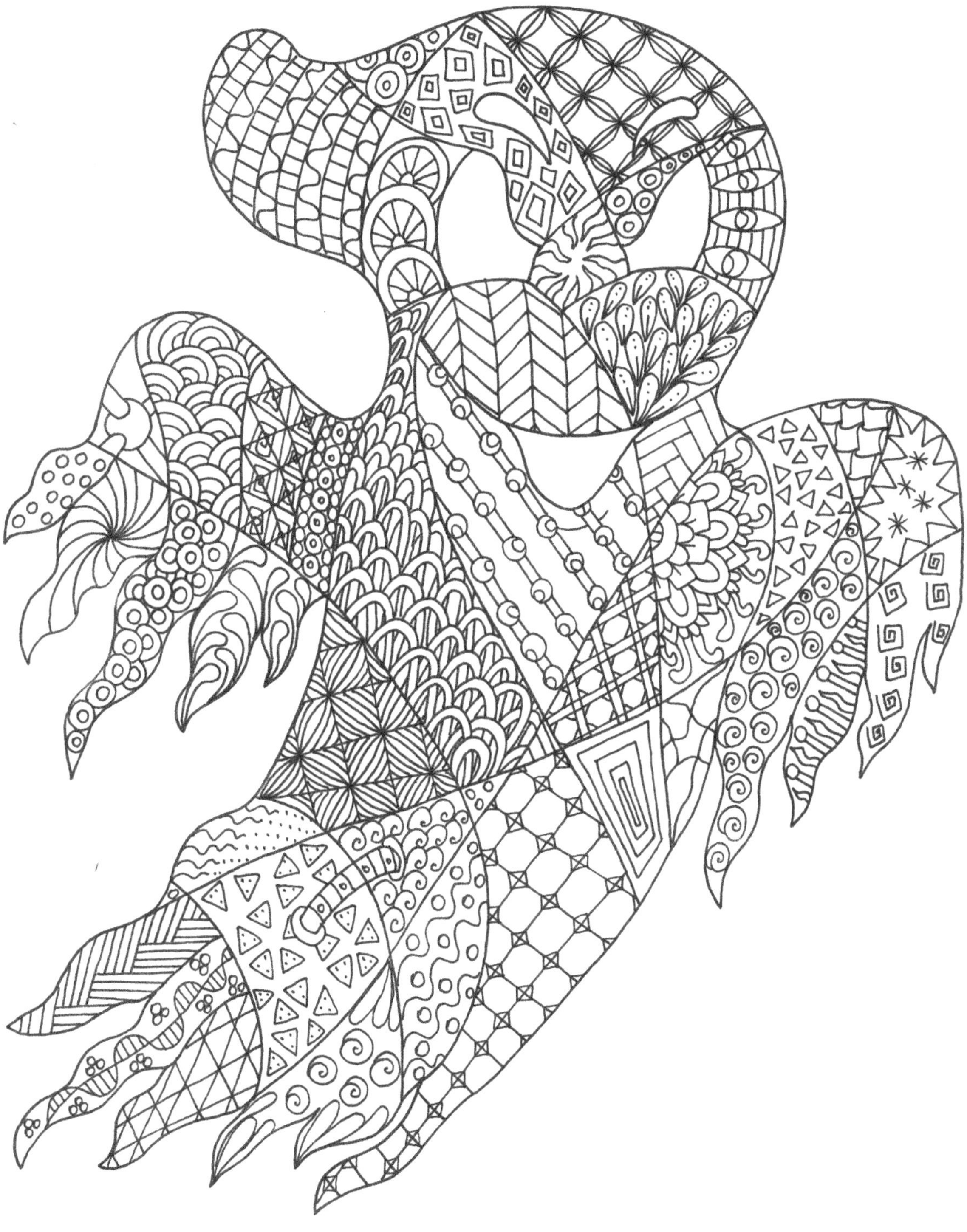

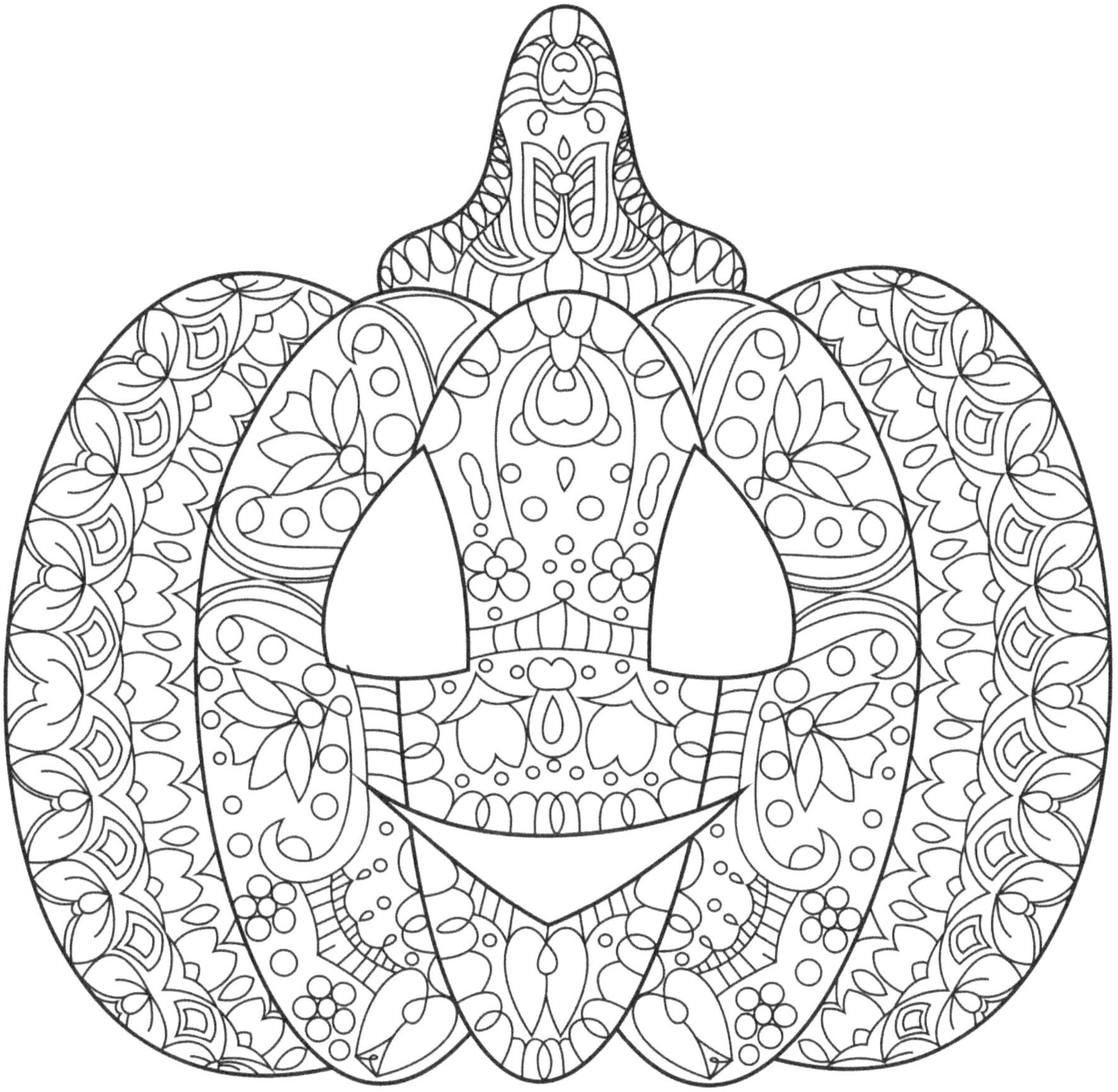

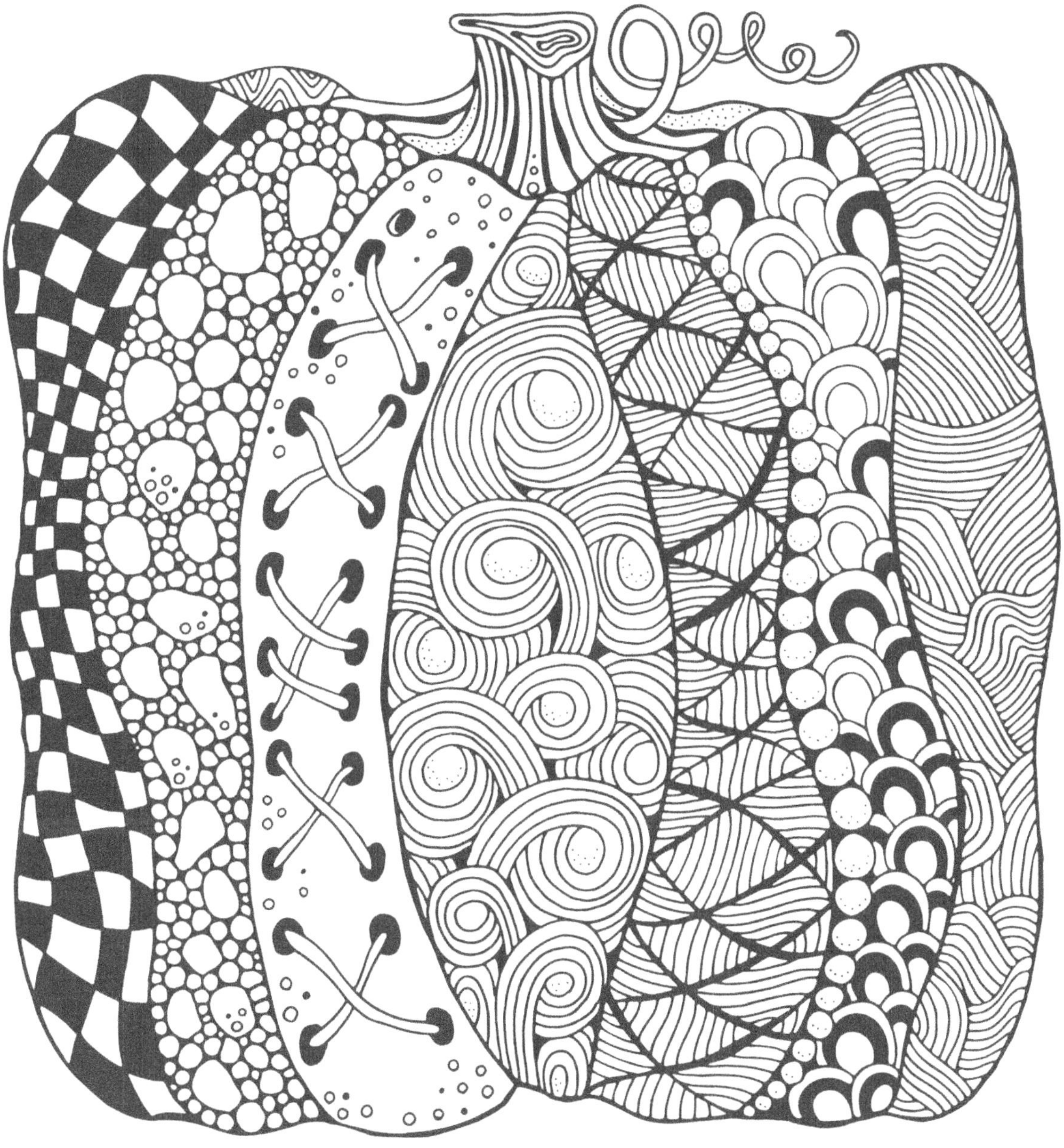

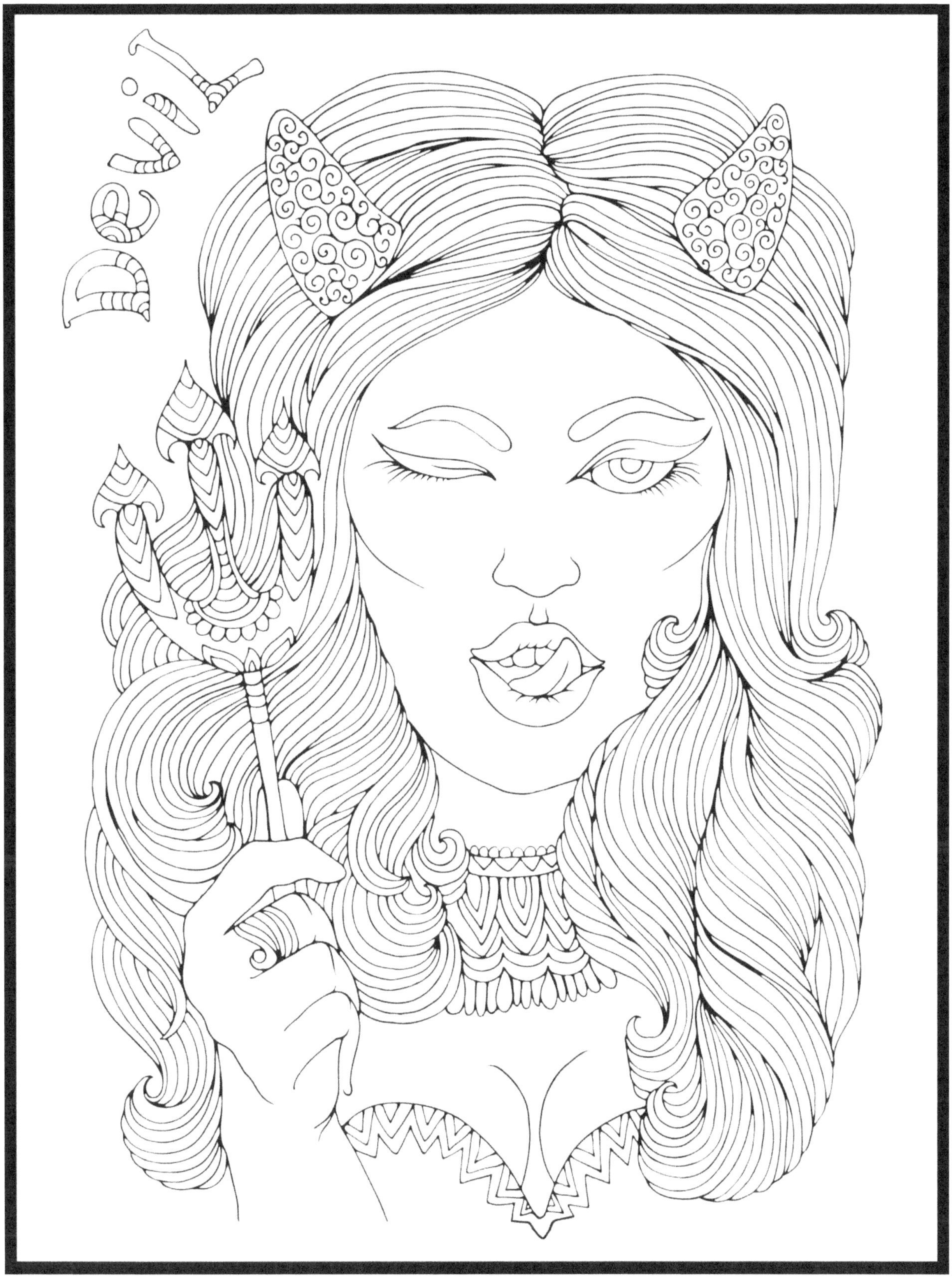
Devil

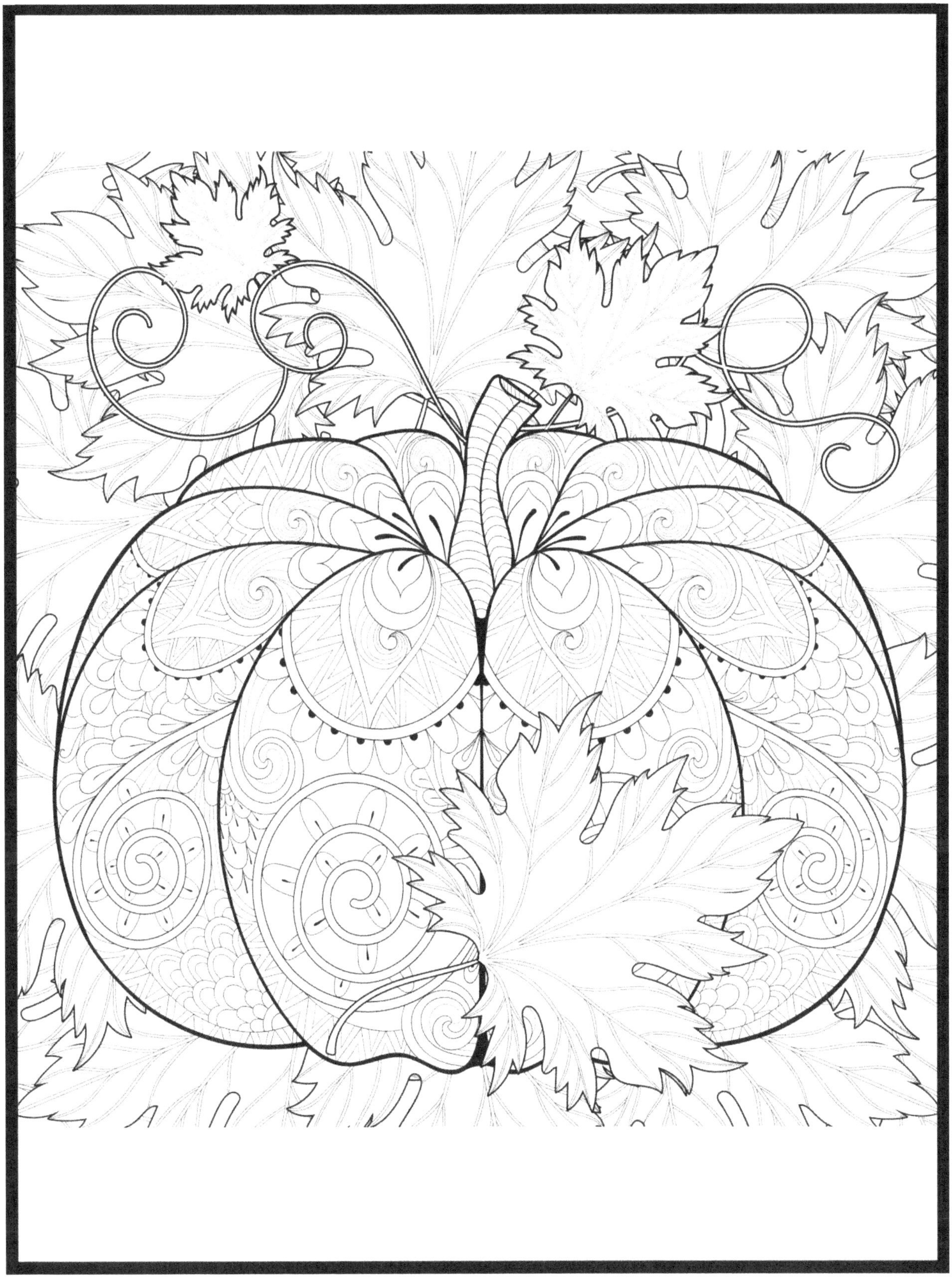

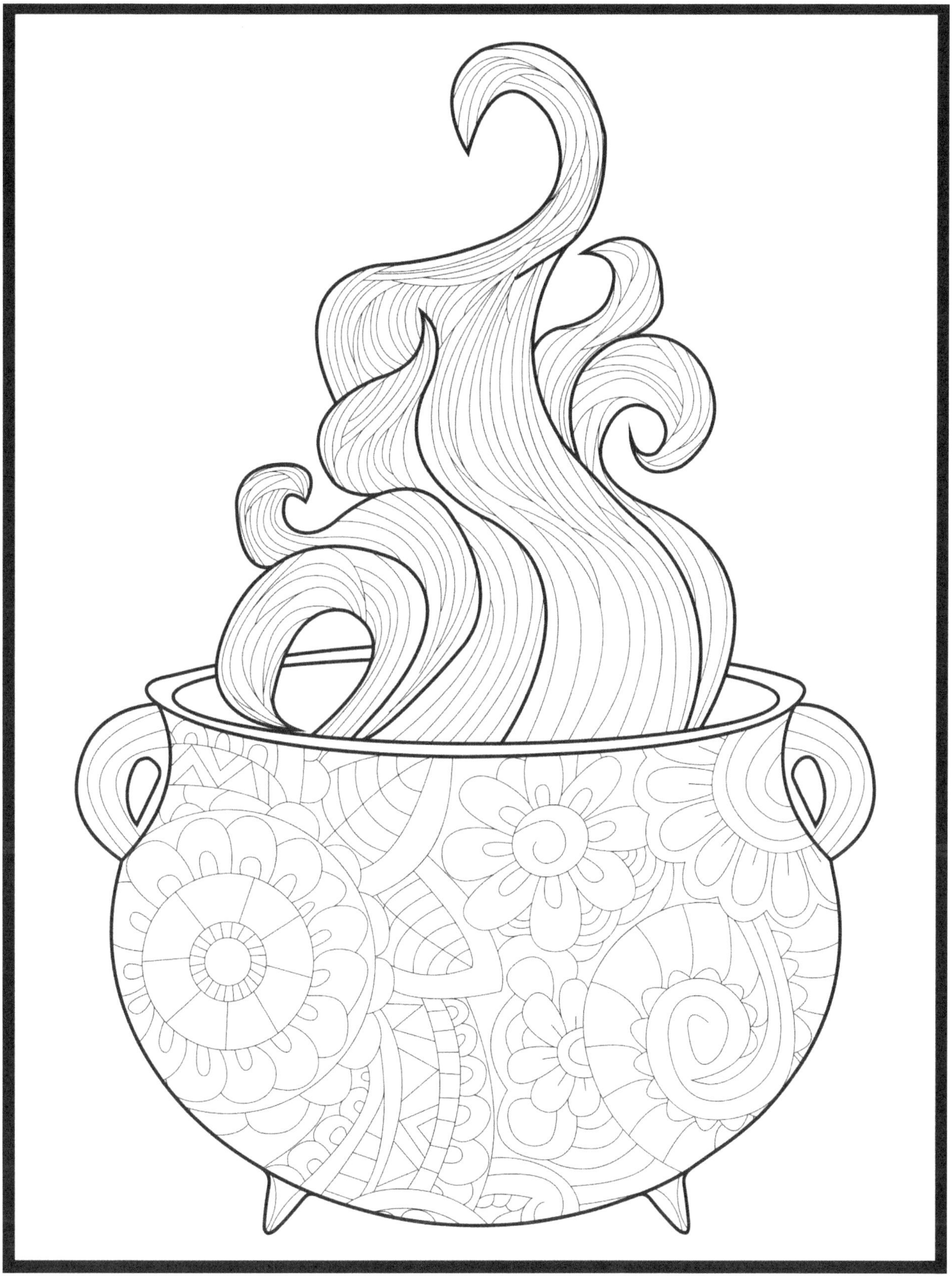

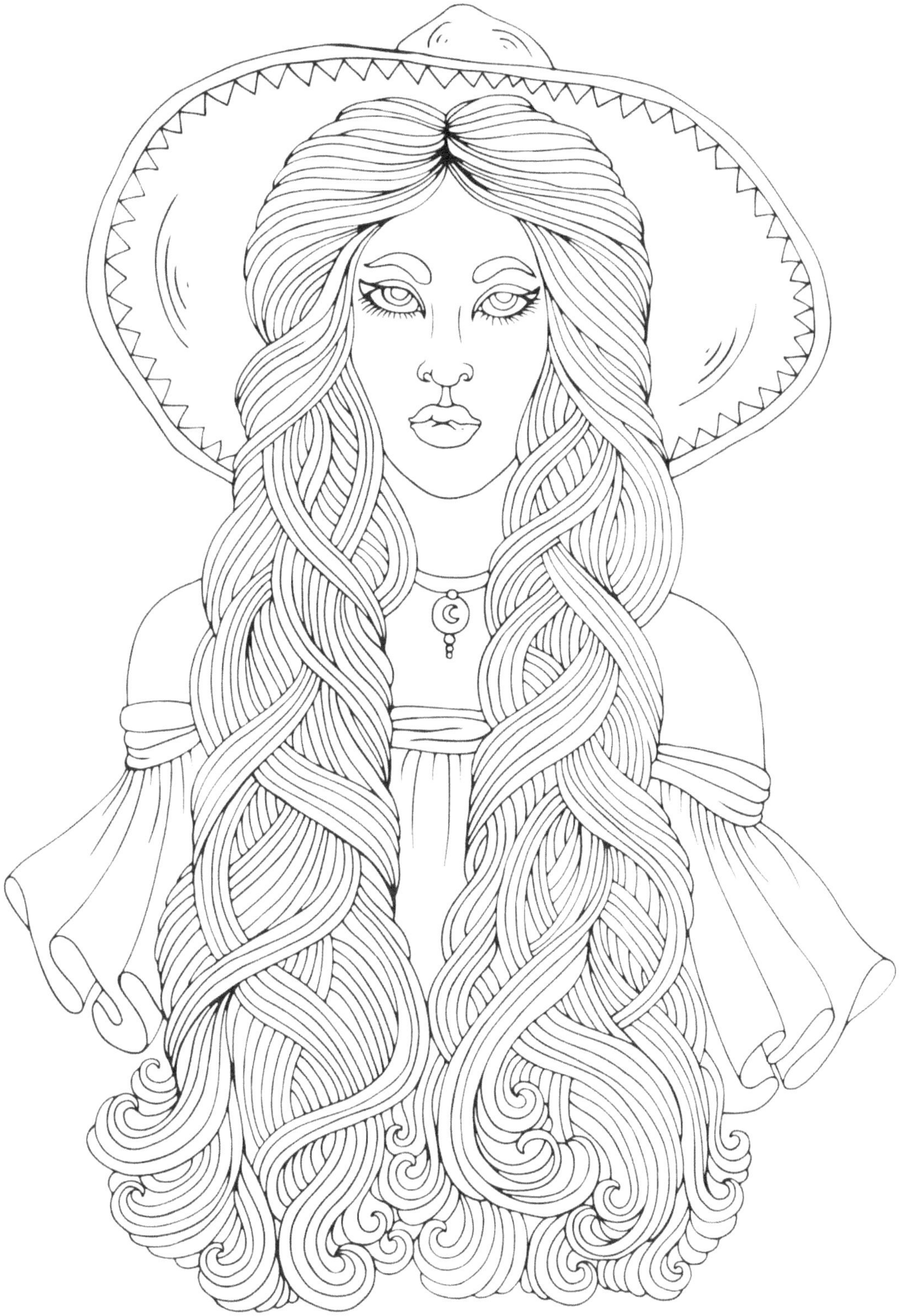

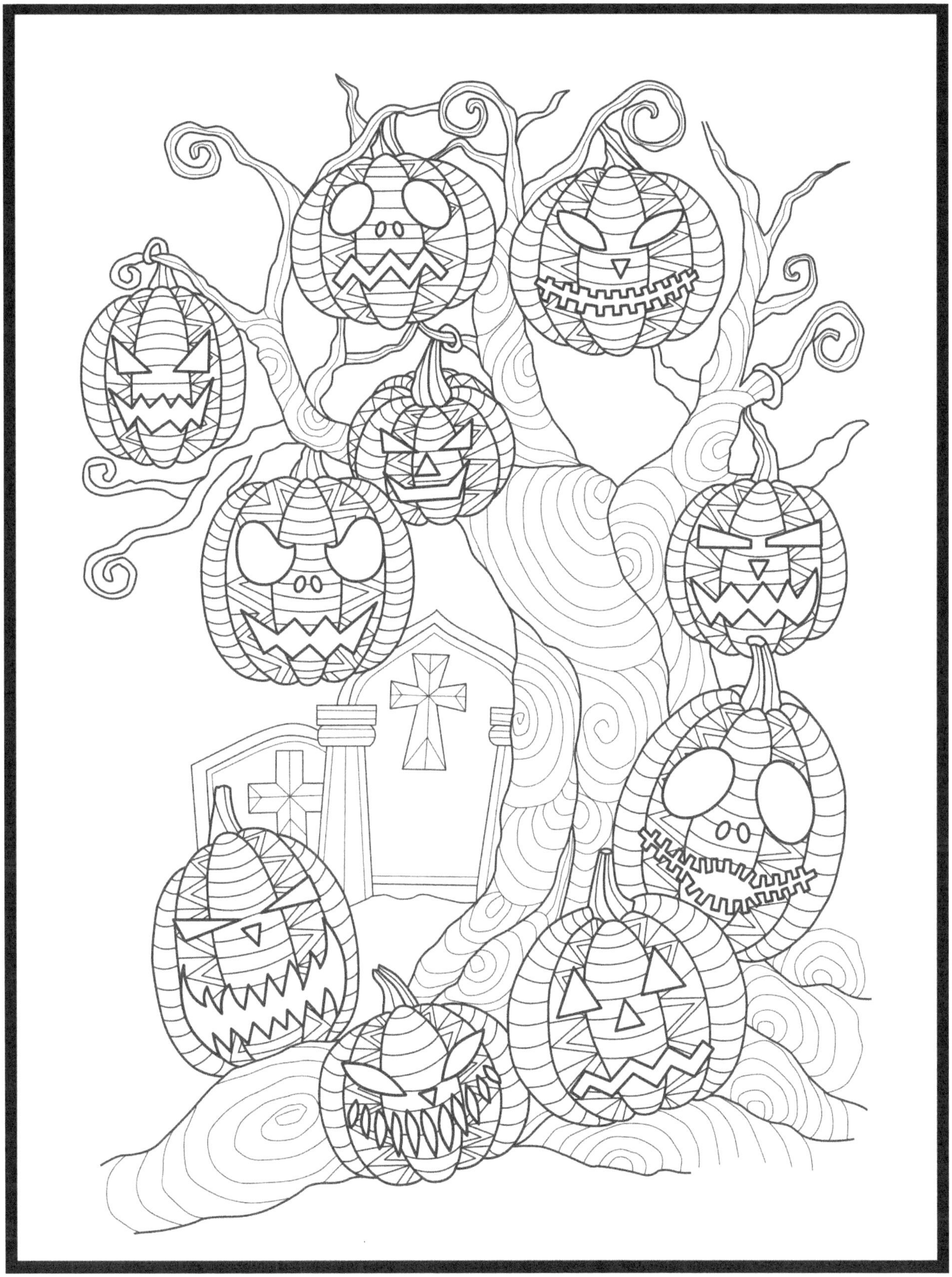

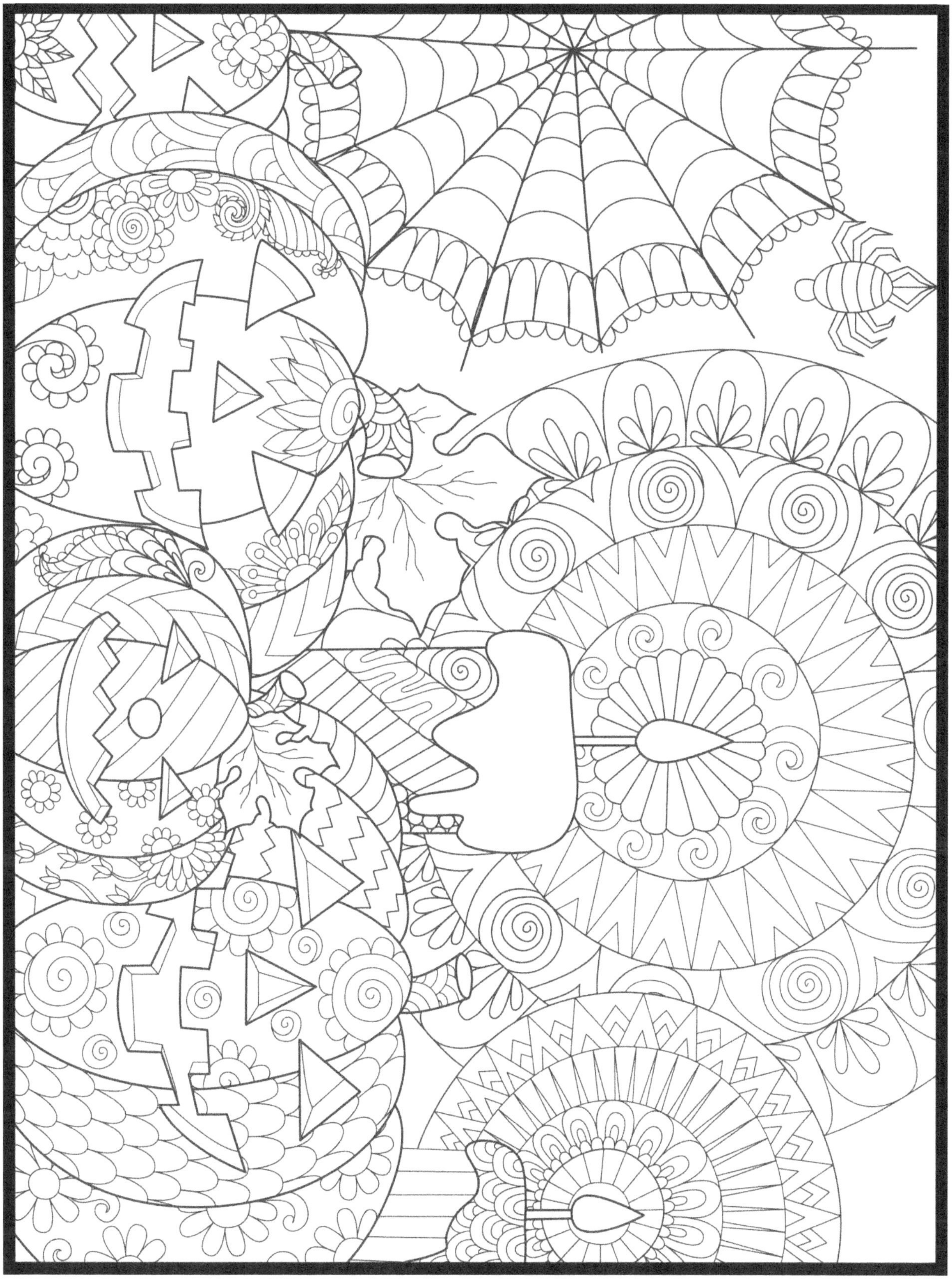

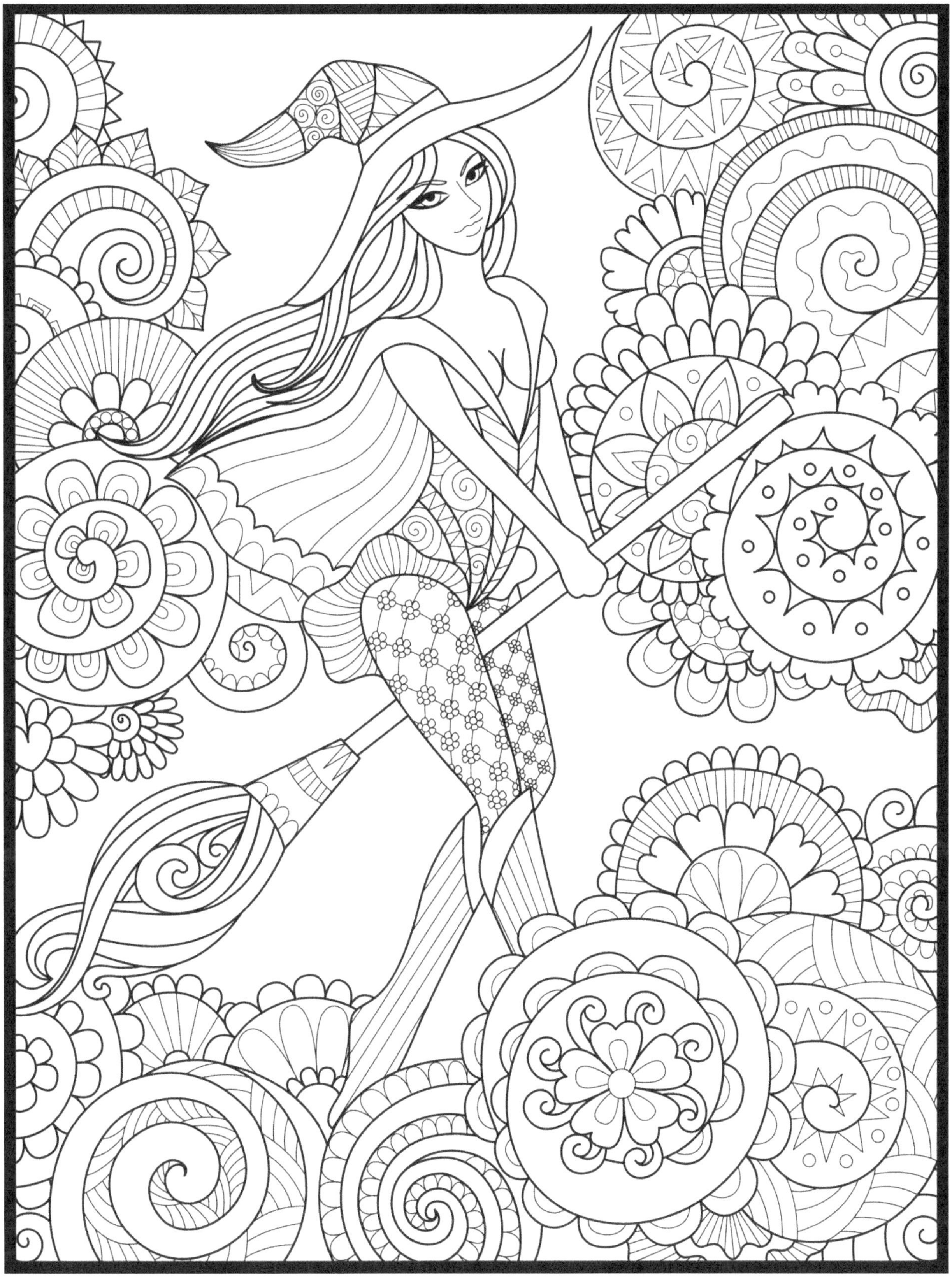

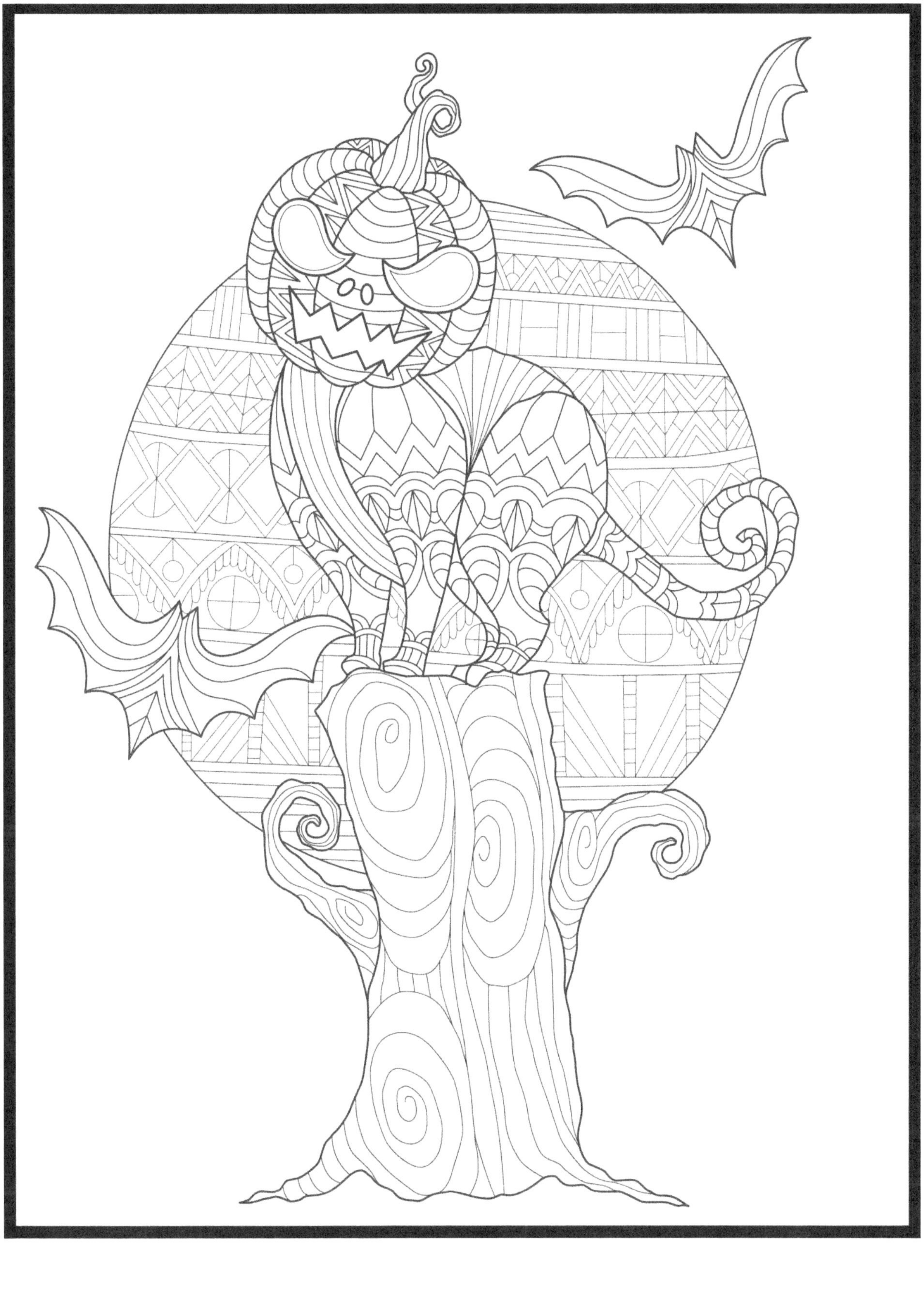

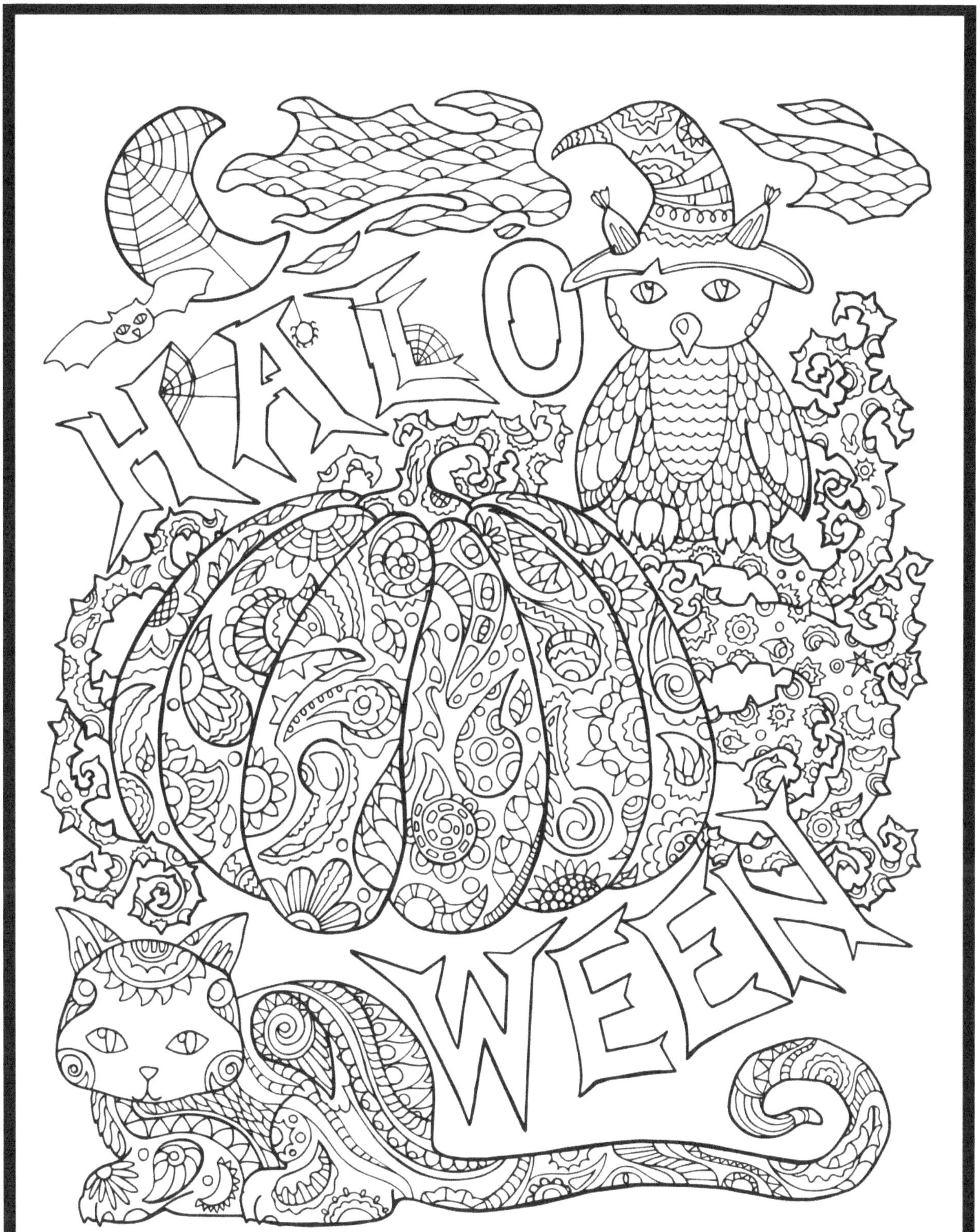
HALO
WEEN

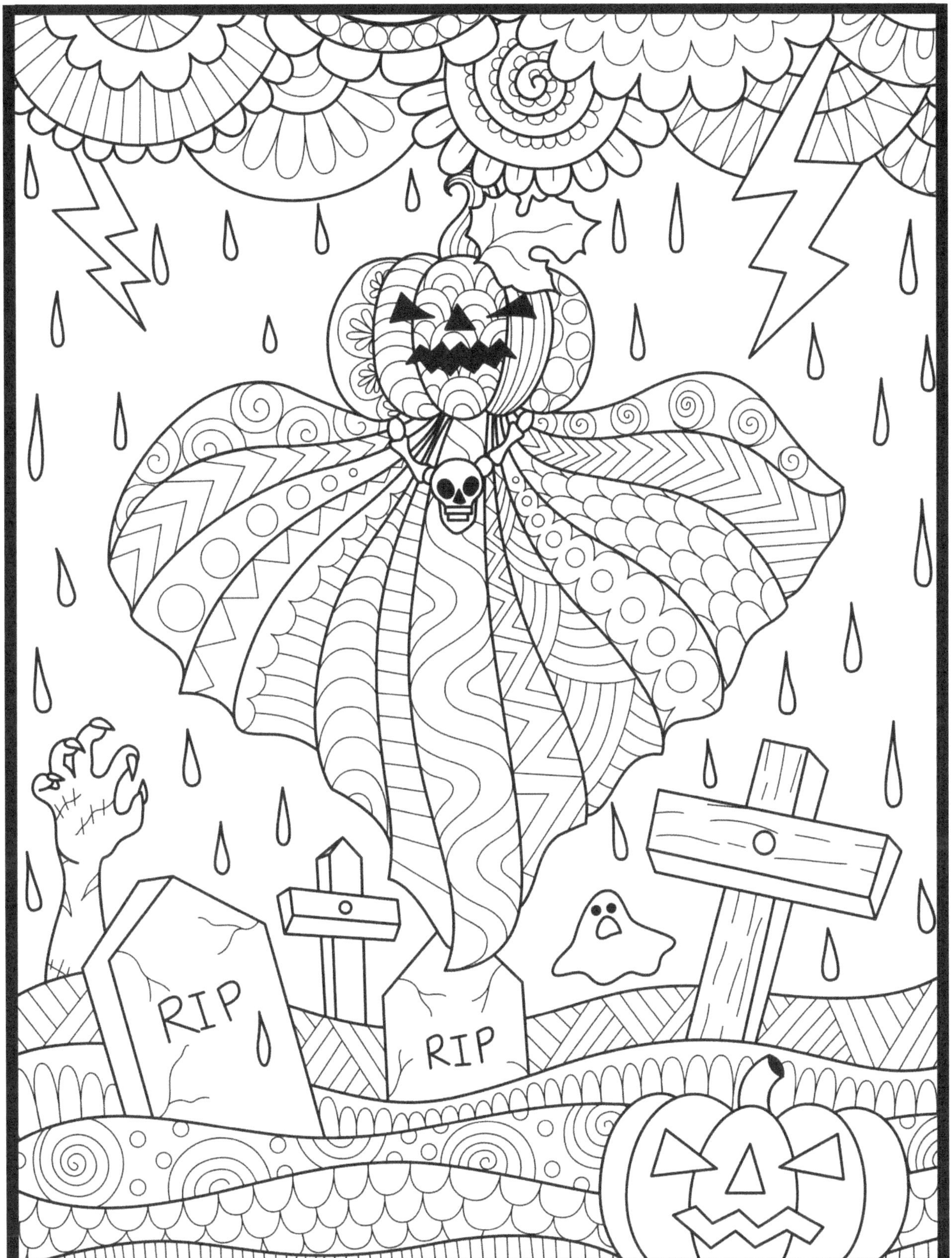
RIP
RIP

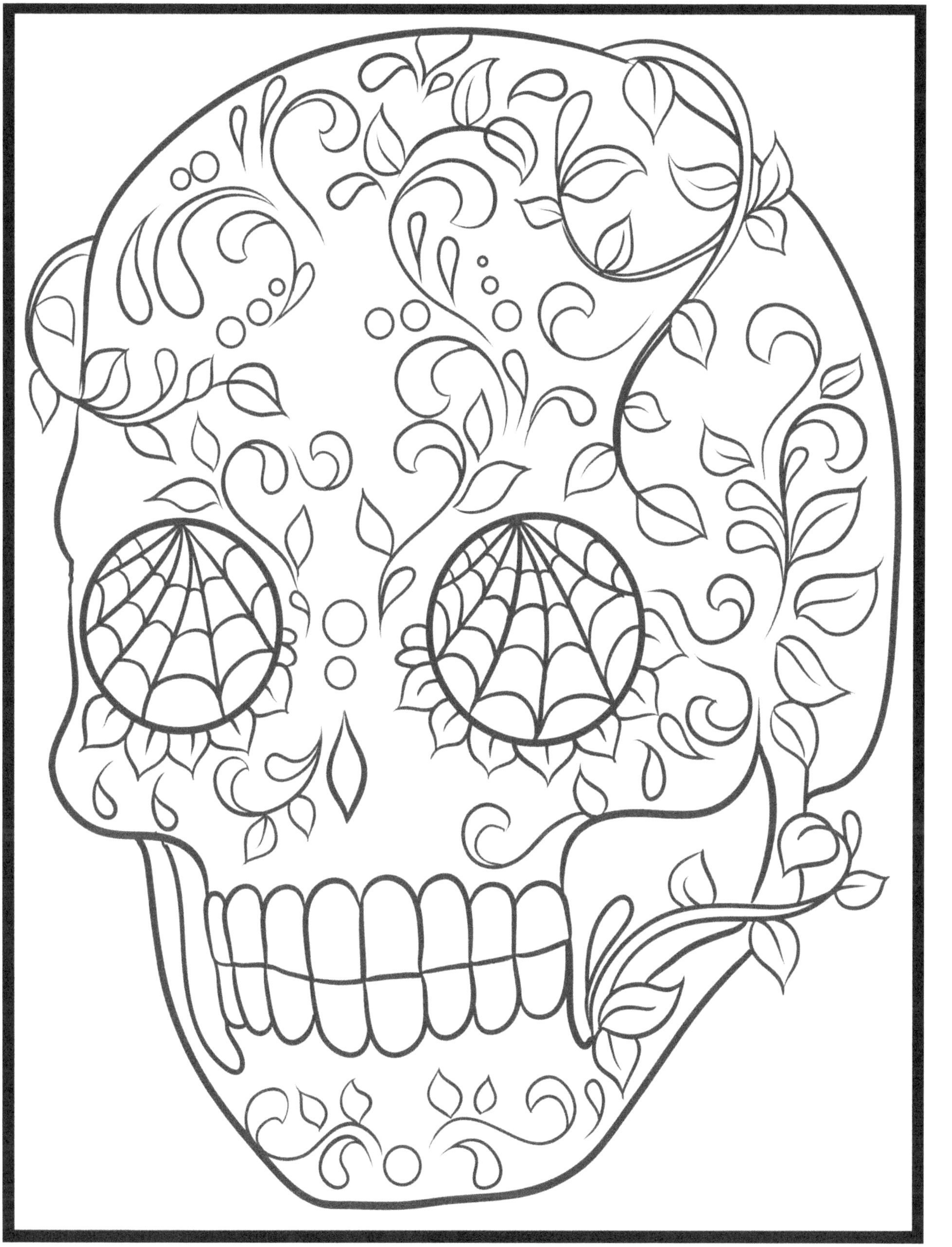

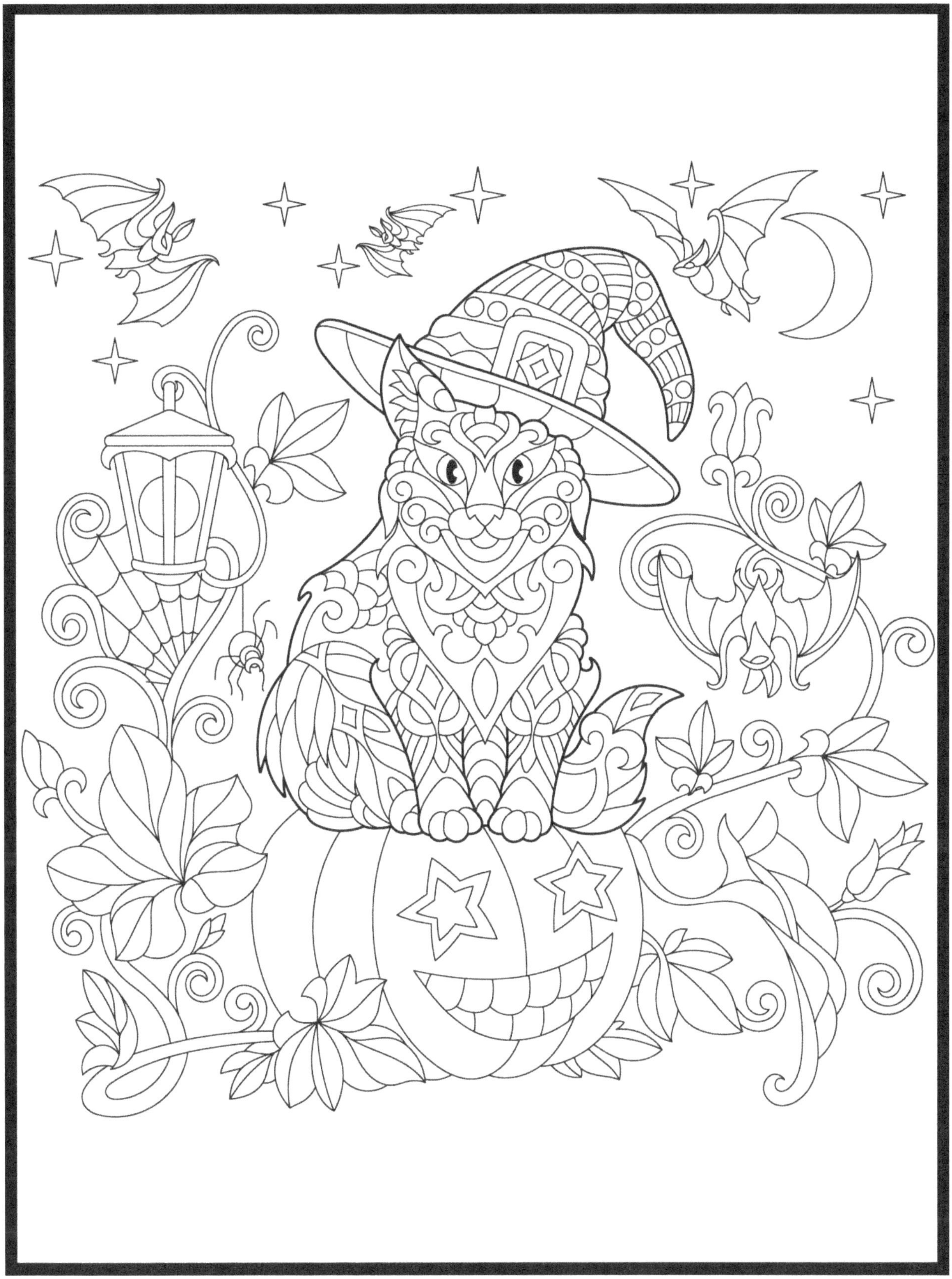

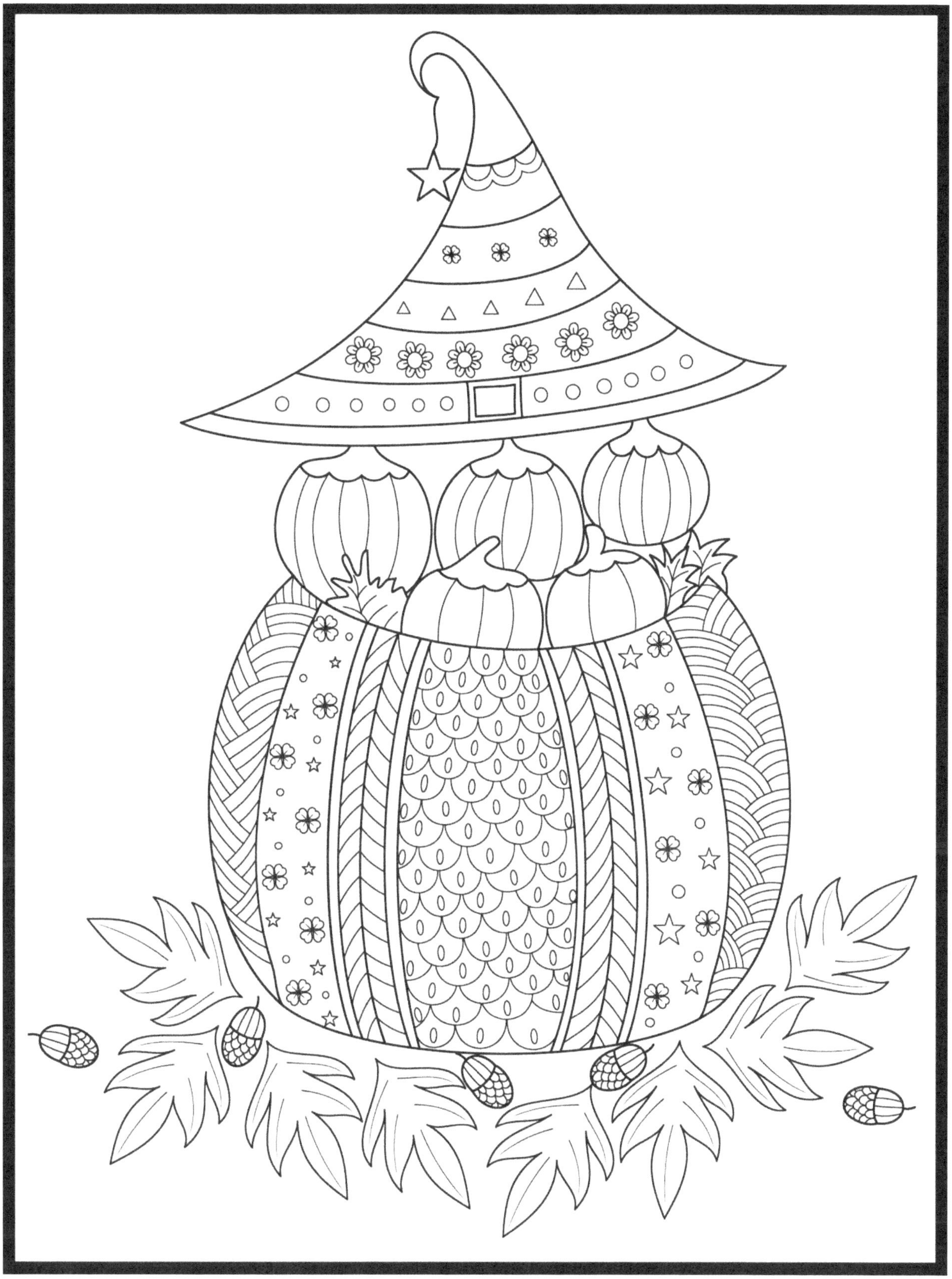

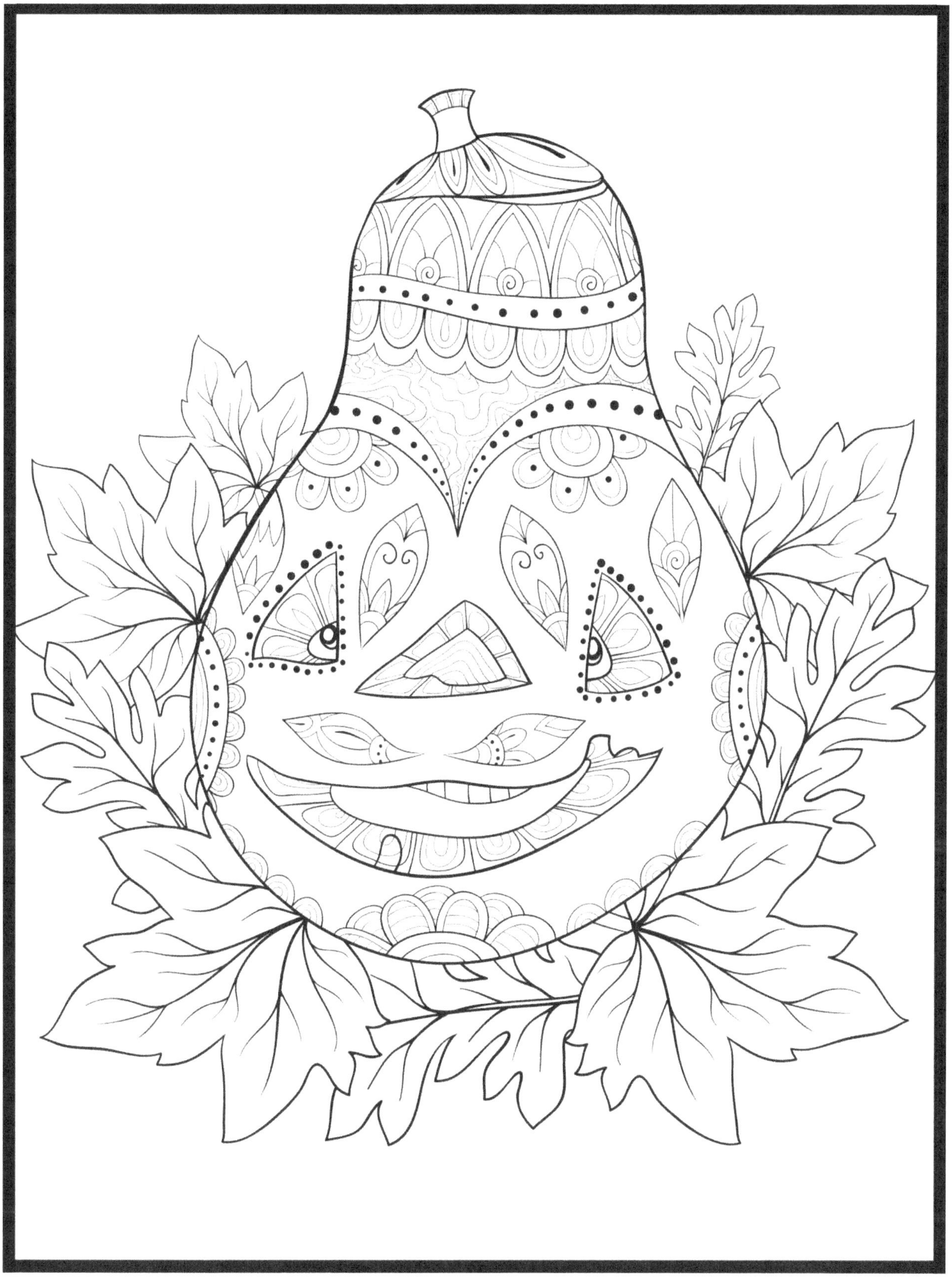

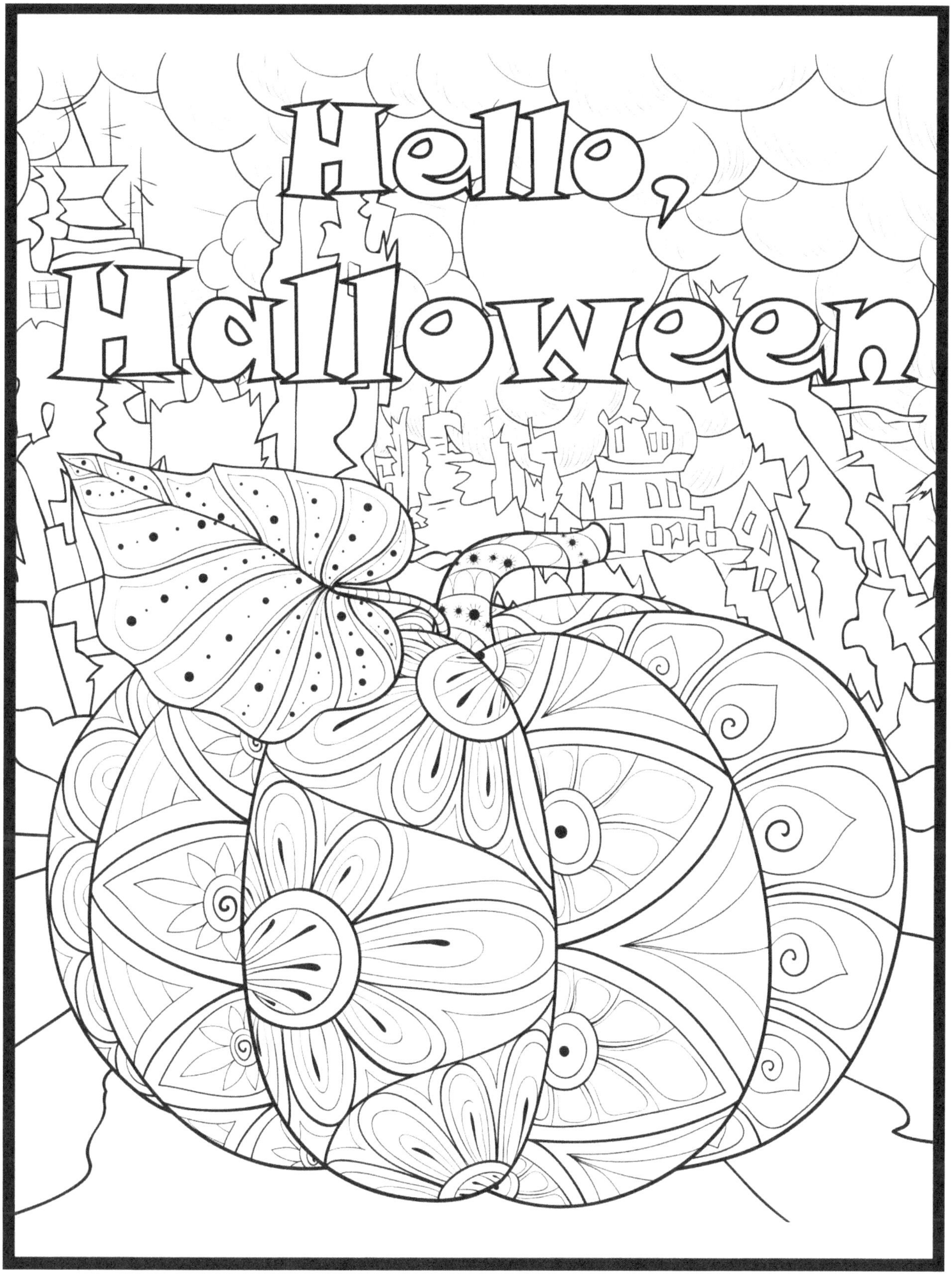
Hello,
Halloween

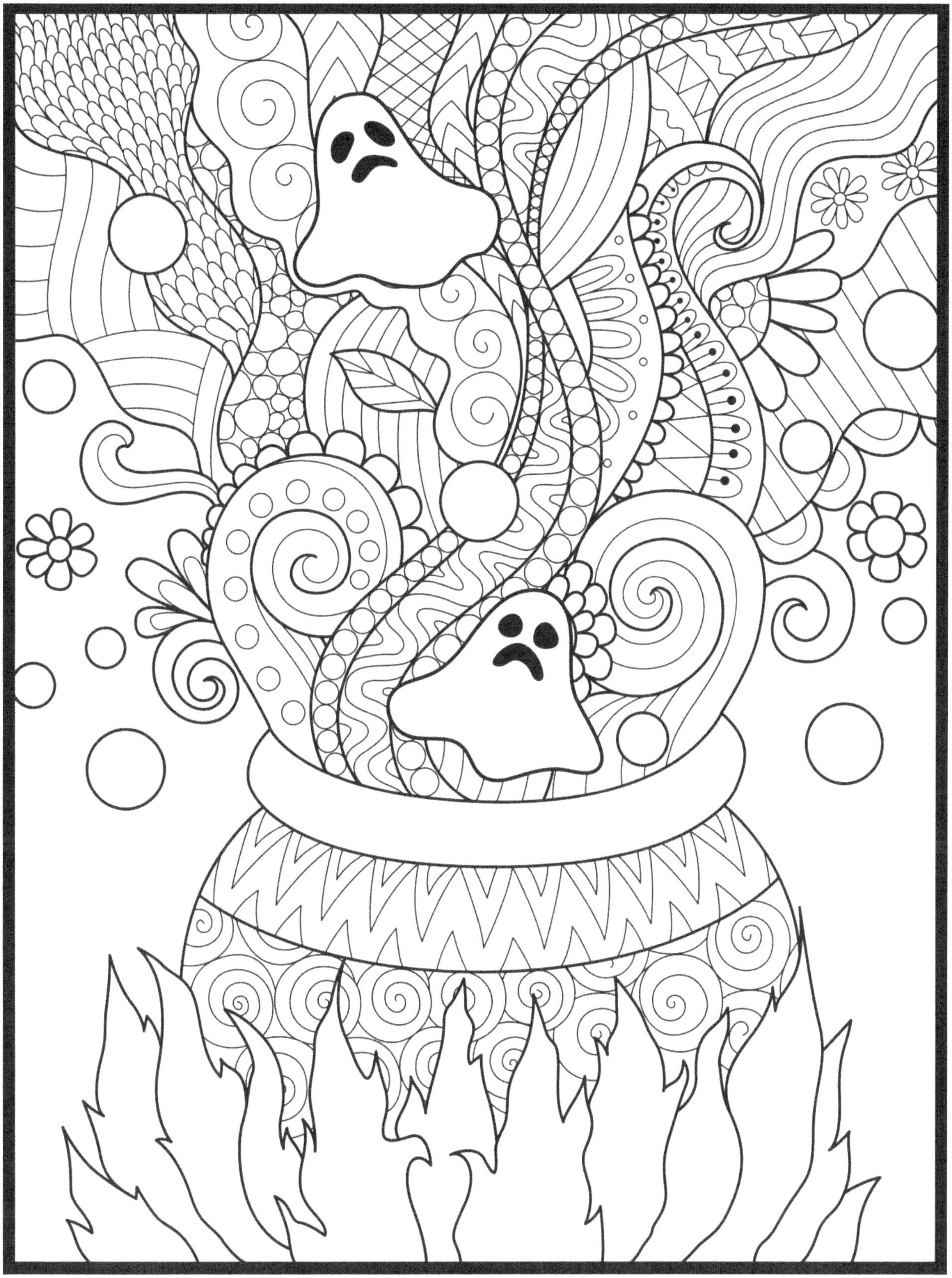

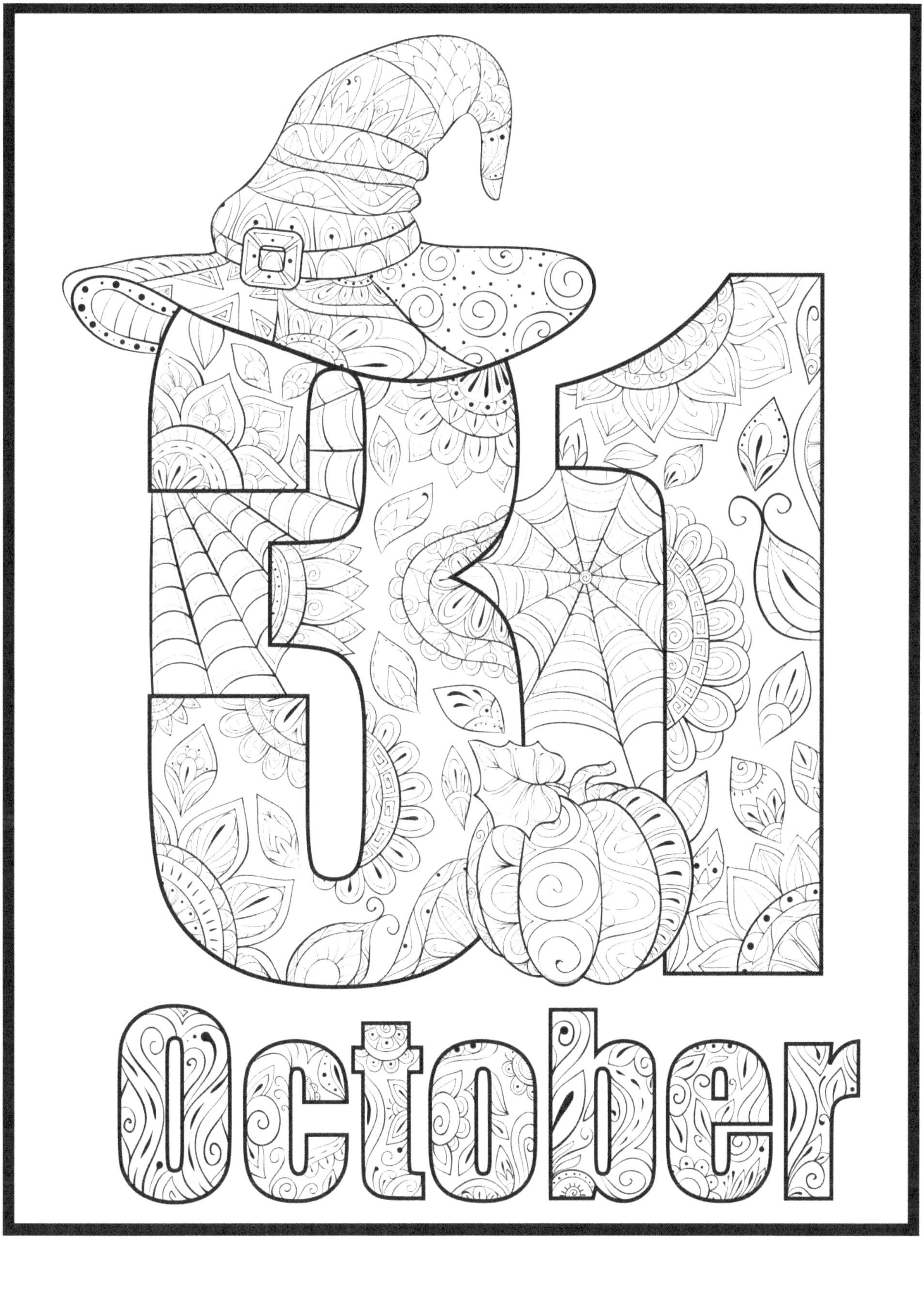
31
October

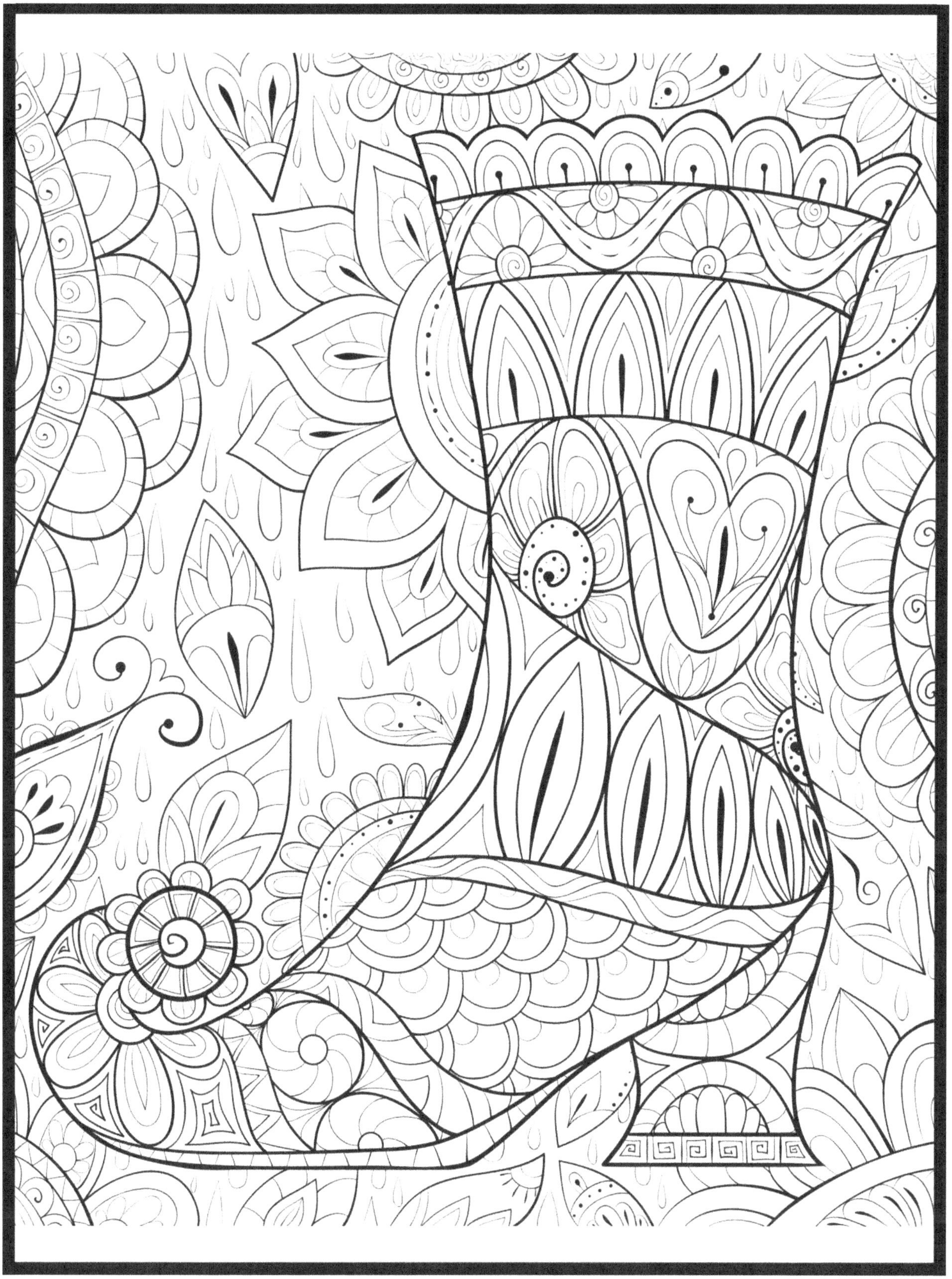

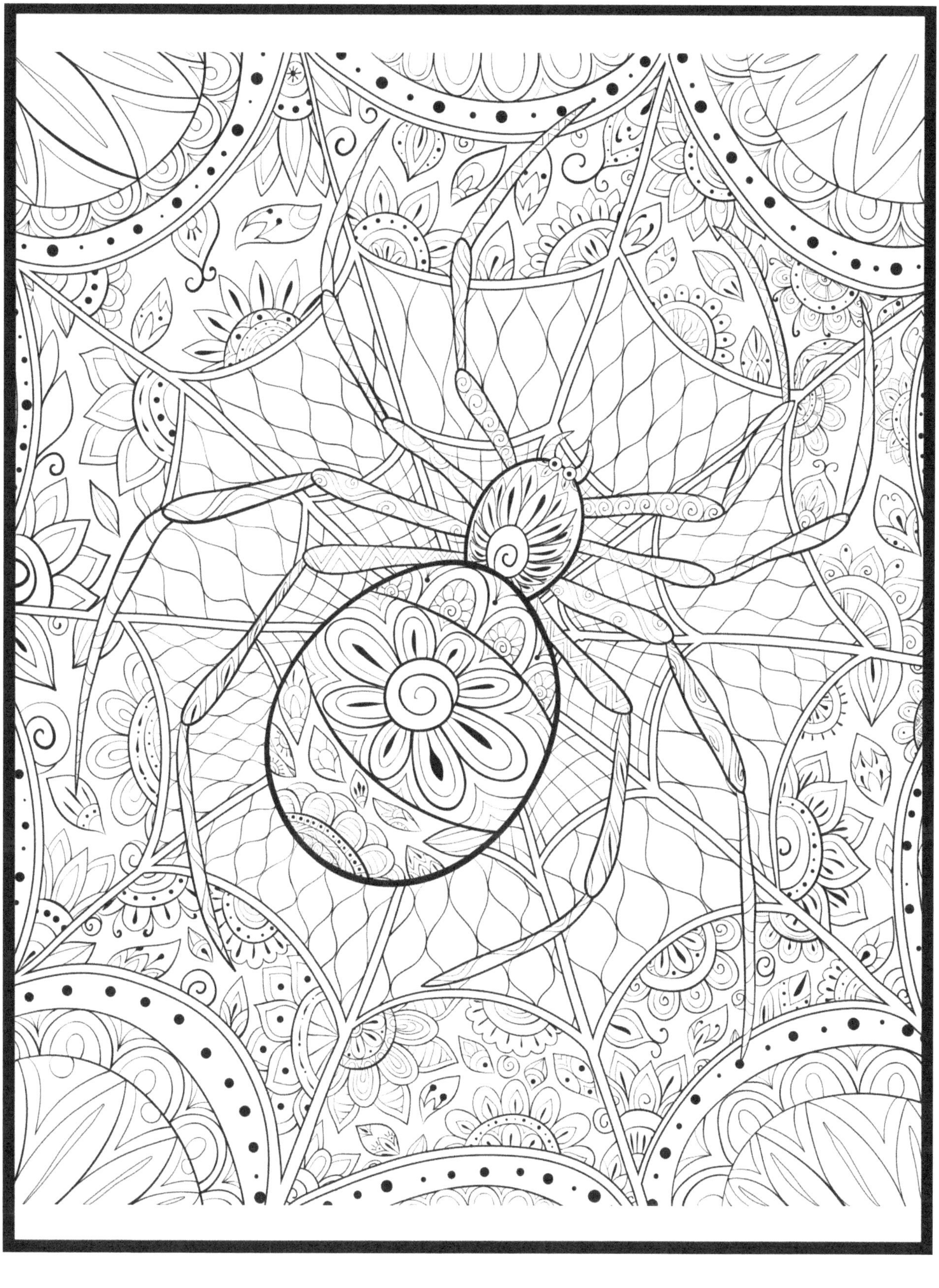

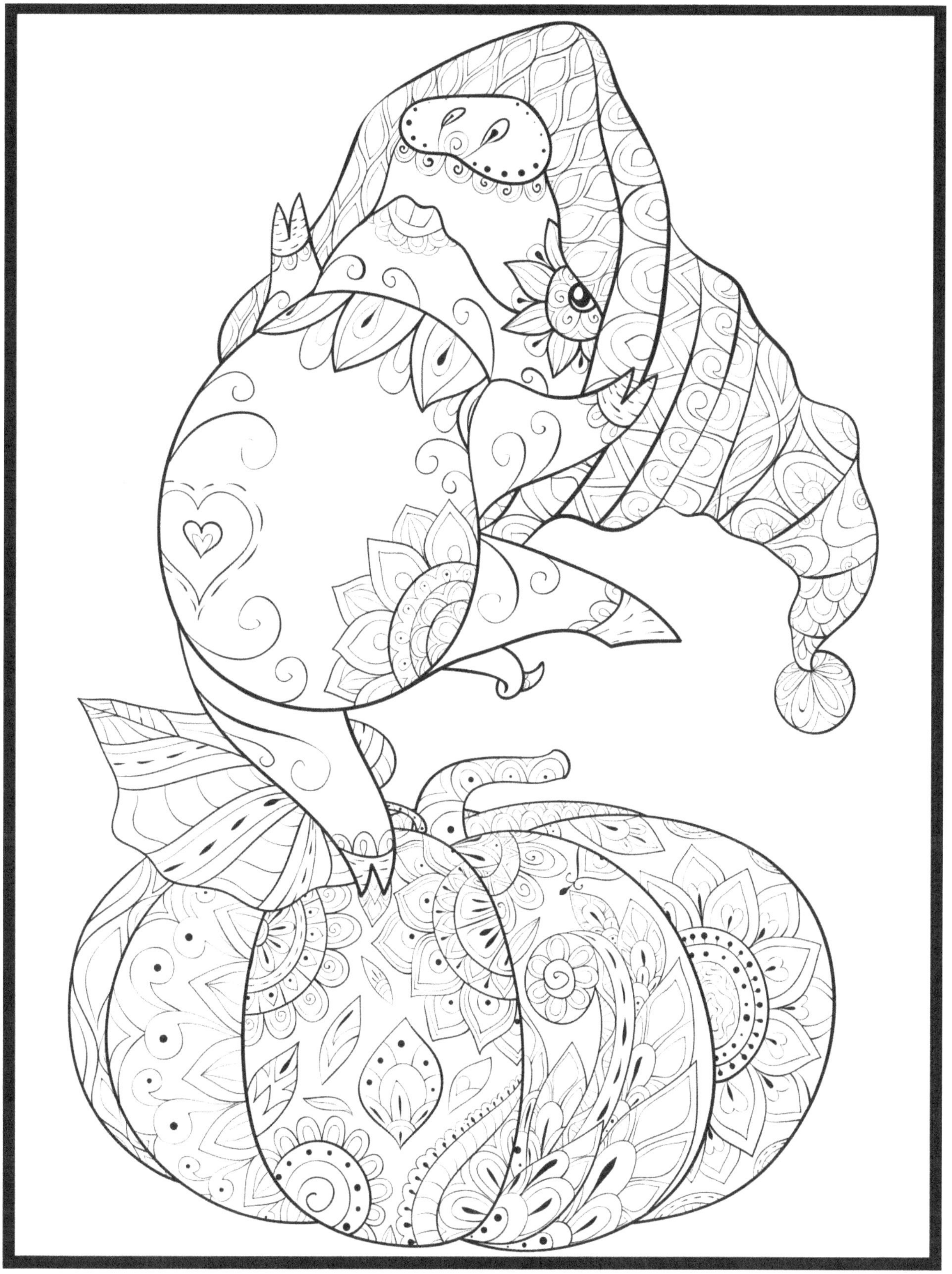

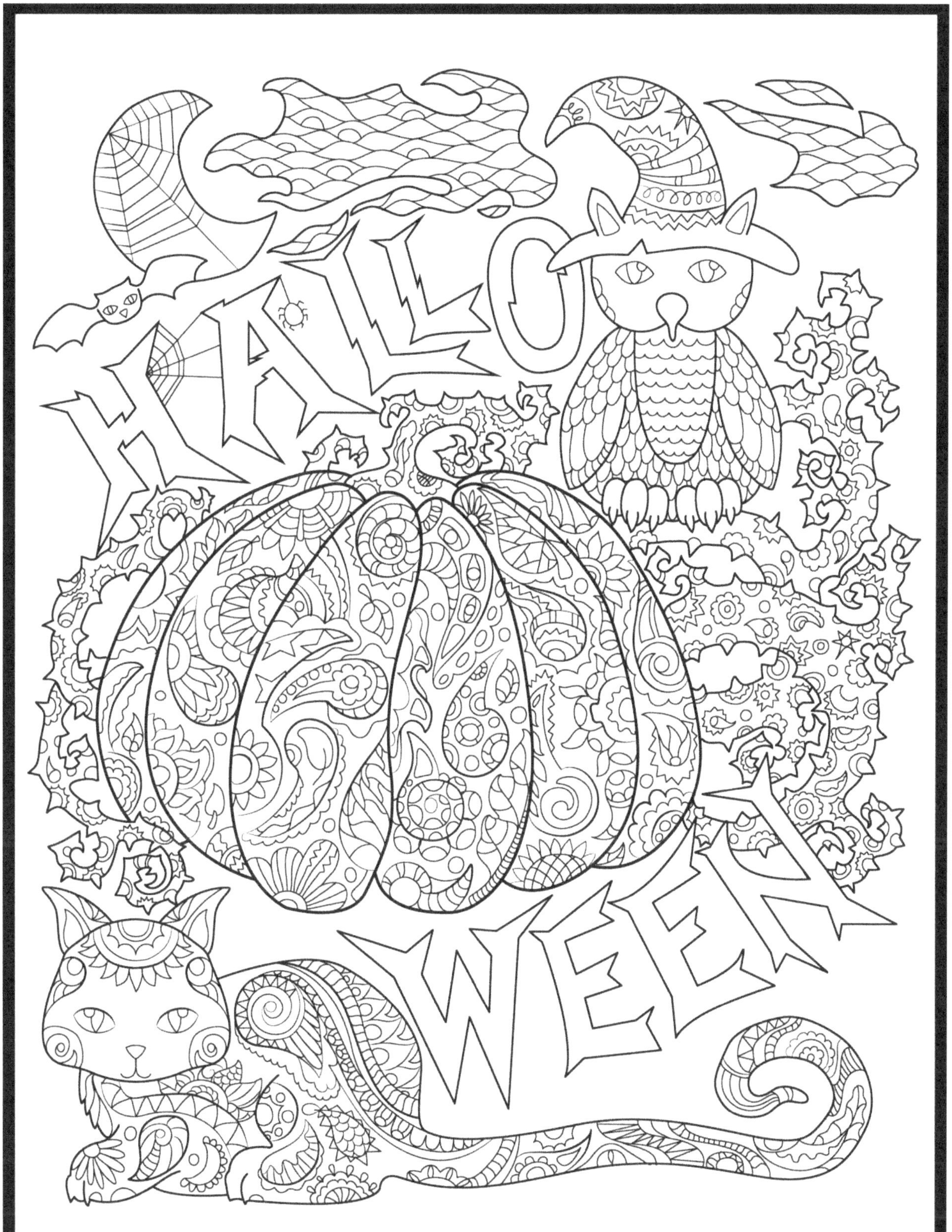
HALLO
WEEN

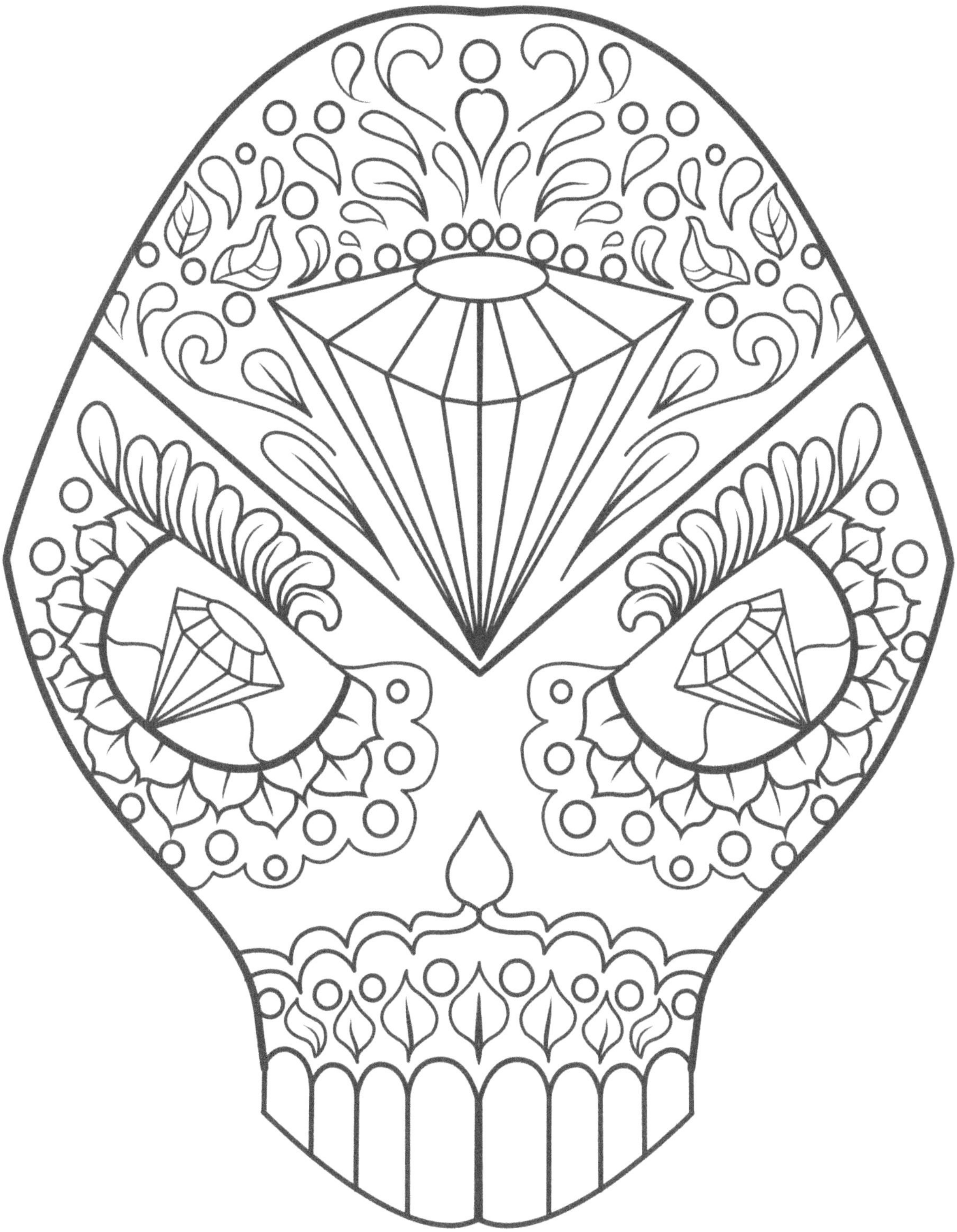

www.ingramcontent.com/pod-product-compliance
Lightning Source LLC
Chambersburg PA
CBHW082252220526
45469CB00009B/2972
* 9 7 8 1 7 2 6 3 9 9 8 1 4 *